SSI MONOGRAPH

CENTRAL ASIAN SECURITY TRENDS: VIEWS FROM EUROPE AND RUSSIA

Stephen J. Blank
Editor

April 2011

Published by Books Express Publishing
Books Express, 2011
ISBN 978-1-780395-15-9

Books Express publications are available from all good retail and online booksellers. For
publishing proposals and direct ordering please contact us at: info@books-express.com

CONTENTS

FOREWORD

President Barack Obama has outlined a comprehensive strategy for the war in Afghanistan, which is now the central front of our campaign against Islamic terrorism. That strategy strongly connects our prosecution of that war to our policy in Pakistan and internal developments there as a necessary condition of victory. But it has also provided for a new logistics road through Central Asia. In this monograph, Dr. Blank argues that a winning strategy in Afghanistan depends, as well, upon the systematic leveraging of the opportunity provided by that road and a new coordinated nonmilitary approach to Central Asia. That approach would rely heavily on improved coordination at home and the more effective leveraging of our superior economic power in Central Asia to help stabilize that region so that it provides a secure rear to Afghanistan. In this fashion, we would help Central Asia meet the challenges of extremism, of economic decline due to the global economic crisis, and thus of political stability in states that are likely to be challenged by the confluence of those trends.

This monograph therefore contributes directly to the debate on U.S. strategy in Afghanistan and Central Asia and duly represents a part of the Strategic Studies Institute's continuing efforts to participate in and help shape that debate over U.S. strategy and policy. The topic could not be more timely, and we hope that it will influence those ongoing debates about U.S. strategy in Afghanistan and Central Asia.

DOUGLAS C. LOVELACE, JR.
Director
Strategic Studies Institute

v

INTRODUCTION

On January 25-26, 2010, SSI organized a conference entitled, "Contemporary issues in International Security," at the Finnish embassy in Washington, DC. This was the second in what we hoped will be annual conferences bringing together U.S., European, and Russian scholars and experts to discuss such issues in an open forum. The importance of such regular dialogues among experts is well known, and the benefits of these discussions are considerable. Just as we published the papers of the 2008 conference in 2009 (Stephen J. Blank, ed., *Prospects for U.S.-Russian Security Cooperation*, Carlisle, PA: Strategic Studies Institute, U.S. Army War College, 2009), we are doing so now. However, in this case, we are publishing the papers on a panel-by-panel basis.

The papers collected in this volume pertain to Central Asia. Indeed, they offer us two foreign views of the strategic situation evolving there—a Russian and a French analysis. For obvious reasons: the war in Afghanistan, proximity to major global actors, large energy holdings, and for less obvious reason, i.e., the possibility that domestic instability in one or more of these states could spread to other Muslim states as we now see in the Arab revolutions of 2011, Central Asia is an increasingly important and interesting strategic region. As such, it merits sustained critical attention and analysis of the sort we are presenting here and that we have presented in the past. We also intend to continue doing so in the future. Yet for all of Central Asia's growing importance, it is a hard area to grasp analytically. To nonspecialists, it is likely to be something of a terra incognita, an unknown region, whose landmarks impart a sense of unfamiliarity, even unease, to those coming from the outside to try and understand it. Yet, at the same time, even for specialists, its reality is elusive and debates abound as to the nature of its domestic politics in both individual states and across the region. Moreover, the question of the stability of either individual states or of the region, a key question for foreign policymakers and analysts, is one of the most contested of the questions currently being debated.

Many analysts have accepted what has become a paradigm: that these states are fundamentally precarious due to internal cleavages between social and ethnic groups, face potentially devastating environmental and economic hazards, are fundamentally misgoverned autocracies that will inevitably explode sooner or later, and carry within them the threat of Islamic fundamentalist and terrorist forces coming to power as a result of pervasive misrule.

However, more recently it has become clear that Central Asian governments (not surprisingly) resent this characterization of their efforts and point to 20 years of stability—often against all predictions—as testimony for their capacity for growth and stability. Obviously, we cannot give a definitive answer to these questions in the space of a single collection of essays. But the point of these essays, and of the panel from which they have sprung, is to encourage our readers to take a more lively interest in this region whose strategic future is increasingly entangled with U.S. interests and those of key allies and other major international actors. As September 11, 2001, showed, threats originating here can reach out and touch the United States. Certainly they can also reach out to Europe as subsequent terror attacks show. For this reason, we hope that the essays presented here, as well as our previous efforts to understand trends in this region and what will be future publications along this line, will help to enlighten policymakers and planners, as well as specialists and other readers about the growing importance of the region and the increased necessity of obtaining a deeper understanding of its evolution.

Professor Stephen Blank
Strategic Studies Institute

CHAPTER 1

RUSSIA-CENTRAL ASIA: ADVANCES AND SHORTCOMINGS OF THE MILITARY PARTNERSHIP

SÉBASTIEN PEYROUSE

INTRODUCTION

The classic external security threats are fewer in Central Asia: all the bordering states have recognized their respective independence and make no territorial claims in their regards. Russia has never threatened the Central Asian states with any sort of military intervention related to border issues. Territorial conflicts with China were settled on friendly terms, and Russia's southern borders with Iran and Afghanistan were not put into question after the disappearance of the Soviet Union. Only the maritime borders of the Caspian Sea remain the object of continuing debate, in particular those between Turkmenistan and Iran, and Turkmenistan and Azerbaijan. The militarization of the Caspian Sea, especially the development of a Kazakh naval fleet, is intended to respond not to classic military attacks, but to nontraditional threats, including the possible perpetration of terrorist attacks on oil rigs and tankers; the protection of commercial ships crossing the sea; the struggle against poaching sturgeon; and the management of emergency climatic situations.[1] Security threats therefore exist either between the Central Asian states themselves—these mainly concern water management issues—or are related to nontraditional threats. Indeed, it is necessary to have a broad definition of security for Central Asia, one that is distinct from the traditional, state-centric view that centers on military issues—weak states and/or economies, unresolved conflicts, pauperization, migration, organized crime, drug trafficking, and corruption—but also terrorism, Islamist insurrectionist movements, energy security, nuclear proliferation, chemical and biological weapons, maritime security, the environment, health (pandemics), and food security. All these concerns reveal the existence of forms of low-intensity conflict and failures in governance.

What is Russia's role in the securitization of Central Asia? Since the early 1990s, this strategic domain has been the driving force behind Moscow's continued presence in the region; however, since 2000, the mechanisms and magnitude of this collaboration have been profoundly transformed. The Central Asian states were led, more often grudgingly than out of conviction, gradually to increase their cooperation with the former metropole. This is especially important as the establishing of relations of confidence with other partners (the United States, the European Union [EU], China, Turkey, or India) in a sector as crucial as the military has turned out to be more complex than predicted. In addition, the ability of the governments to coordinate any intra-Central Asian military cooperation has worked in favor of Russia's continuing role as the privileged partner of the national armies, in a bilateral as much as multilateral framework. All the same, Russia no longer enjoys its former monopoly over the now open market of Central Asian military cooperation, and its responses to nontraditional dangers are above all conventional ones.

THE EVOLVING ROLE AND PLACE OF RUSSIA IN THE CENTRAL ASIAN SECURITY SYSTEM

From the fall of the Soviet Union to the mid 1990s, the Kremlin was without any clear Central Asian policy. Moscow retained a partial interest in the region only in the strategic domain, which involved renting the site of the Baikonur Cosmodrome in Kazakhstan; putting political pressure on the new states to ensure compliance with the Commonwealth for Independent States (CIS) Collective Security Treaty signed in May 1992; maintaining Russian troops in Kyrgyzstan, Tajikistan, and Turkmenistan along the international borders with China, Afghanistan, and Iran; and deploying the Russian 201st Motor Rifle Division in Tajikistan during their civil war (1992-97). Moscow very quickly became concerned about possible destabilizations coming from Iran (border with Turkmenistan), from China (borders with Kazakhstan, Kyrgyzstan, and Tajikistan), and obviously from Afghanistan (borders with Turkmenistan, Uzbekistan, and Tajikistan). Only Kazakhstan and Uzbekistan refused Russian military aid for the management of their southern borders upon becoming independent, but for different reasons.[2]

Subsequent to the declarations of independence, Tajikistan was the first Central Asian state to openly call for the maintenance of Russian troops on its territory. The country hosted the 201st Division, called Gachinskaia, which was founded in 1943 and set up in Dushanbe, then Stalinabad, at the end of World War II. It formed one of the contingents of Soviet troops sent to Afghanistan between 1980 and 1989.[3] According to the Russo-Tajik agreement of 1992, the districts of the former Soviet border forces were reorganized, and their jurisdiction transferred to the Special Task Group of the Federal Border Service (GRBTT). This measure was criticized by some experts because it transformed the Russian soldiers responsible for protecting Tajikistan against possible terrorist attacks into immigration or customs offices with a mission to halt the development of smuggling.[4] In 1993, Moscow and Dushanbe signed a friendship, cooperation, and mutual assistance treaty, making it possible to regularize the Russian presence in Tajikistan. At the beginning of the civil war, Russian troops numbered 7,000 men, but their numbers were doubled in 1994. The 201st Division was then assisted by the CIS peacekeeping forces, which involved Russian soldiers but also some Central Asian battalions. In 1994 and 1995, Russian and Central Asian authorities requested that the CIS troops be recognized as peacekeeping troops under United Nations (UN) jurisdiction, which elicited numerous debates as the 201st Division fought against the Tajik Islamic-democratic opposition alongside the Communists of Khudjand and Kuliab, and could not therefore be considered as a neutral force.[5]

In total, about 14,000 military personnel under Russian command served in Tajikistan, 20 percent of them being Russians (essentially officers and noncommissioned officers on contract) and 80 percent Tajiks, mainly soldiers. It was thus especially difficult for Tajikistan to constitute an independent military force, as most of the Tajik officers had preferred to serve as Russian troops given the significant differences in salary. After the peace accords of June 1997, the presence of the CIS forces, whose first mission was to prevent the reprise of conflict between belligerents and to disarm the regional militias, was put into question. In 1999, an agreement on the status of the Russian military presence in Tajikistan brought the withdrawal of the latter but maintained the troops of the 201st Division, whose mission was no longer the domestic political stabilization but solely the securitization of the external borders. As of 2002, President Emomali Rakhmon sought to affirm his authority over the whole of the territory and to normalize the country by presenting it as capable of taking control over its own borders. The polemics with Moscow over the financing of the Russian troops, equally shared between both parties, deteriorated from year to year, with each seeking to reduce its own costs. The Tajik army then sought to take gradual control over the borders first by adopting surveillance tasks over the 500 kilometers (km) with China, then over the borders with Kyrgyzstan. In 2004, the Russian soldiers started to hand over to the Tajiks the responsibility of guarding the 1,400 km of border with Afghanistan. The border zone of Pamir was the first to be retroceded, followed by sections under command of the Moscow and Piandj border battalions, considered particularly strategic in drug-trafficking related issues. This process ended in the fall of 2005. At the occasion of this transfer, Russia left the Tajik border guards with material worth the equivalent of 10 million dollars and transferred the Federal Security Service (FSB) Training Center at Dushanbe, which provides specialized training (snipers, cynologists, explosives specialists, etc.), to the Tajik army.[6]

Russian troops were also present in Kyrgyzstan and Turkmenistan during the 1990s, albeit to a lesser extent and for a shorter duration. In 1992, Kyrgyzstan signed a bilateral treaty on the status of border troops of the Russian Federation situated on the territory of Kyrgyzstan, according to which Moscow took over responsibility of the 1,000 km of the Sino-Kyrgyz border. A joint commandment of the Russo-Kyrgyz border troops was established under Moscow's control.[7] The Russian border guards officially worked in the service of Kyrgyzstan, but in fact, remain subordinated to Russia's border guard agency. They served 5-year contracts and were 80 percent financed by Moscow and 20 percent by Bishkek. Some of these battalions had also welcomed Cossacks from Kyrgyzstan into their ranks.[8] Quickly, this border army of about 3,000 soldiers came to comprise mostly Kyrgyz under the command of the Russian officers. In addition, as of 1994, Kyrgyz soldiers obtained the right to carry out their service with the troops of the Russian Federation either as conscripts or as contract employees. In 1999, after the division of the contested territories was settled between Bishkek and Beijing,[9] the entire control of the border fell under the jurisdiction of the Kyrgyz army. In 2007, several Kyrgyz politicians, including the parliamentary spokesperson, Marat Sultanov, evoked the possibility of the Russian troops returning to the southern borders of the country, but Russia has denied supporting any such initiative.[10]

While Russian military aid to Kyrgyzstan has proceeded without any major political conflict, as relations between Bishkek and Moscow are more or less cordial, Russia's military presence in Turkmenistan has turned out to be more complex and chaotic. With independence, Ashgabat announced the creation of its own border troops in order to put an end to Russian presence, but was hardly capable of establishing an efficient army in such a short time. In 1992, a first bilateral agreement between the two countries placed all border units under Russian-Turkmen leadership for a period of 5 years, during which Moscow had to con-

6

tribute financially to the development of the Turkmen border forces. This unified command was, however, broken off after 1994, although Russia maintained a representative in the Turkmen Defense Ministry and another on the National Security Council. Until this date, Turkmenistan had hosted about 15,000 soldiers under joint Russian-Turkmen command, who were charged with guarding the borders with Iran and Afghanistan. A group of special operations for the Russian border service agency, created in 1994 and numbering between 2,000 and 3,000 men, looked after the protection of the land borders, but also the maritime borders protected by two escort ships with Russian-Turkmen crews. In 1995, an "operational group of Russian border soldiers on the territory of Turkmenistan" was established to support the Turkmen troops. With the rapid deterioration of diplomatic relations between Moscow and Ashgabat, two-thirds of these military personnel left the country in 1996, leaving only 5,000 soldiers remaining in position. In May 1999, Turkmenistan announced its decision to put an end to the treaty of 1993. In December of the same year, all the Russian border guards left the country.[11]

In the 2000s, the key security challenges for Russia in Central Asia became more complex. Any destabilization in the weakest (i.e., Kyrgyzstan, Tajikistan) or the most unstable (i.e., Uzbekistan) states could have immediate repercussions in Russia: Islamist infiltrations in the Volga-Ural region and the North Caucasus, or among migrants; an increase in the inflow of drugs reaching the Russian population, which is already widely targeted by drug traffickers; a loss of control over the export networks of hydrocarbons, over uranium resources, strategic sites in the military-industrial complex, and electricity power stations; a drop in trade exchanges; a loss of direct access to Afghanistan; an uncontrollable surge of flows of migrants, in particular of refugees. For Moscow, the security of the southern borders of Central Asia is seen as a question of domestic security, though not for reasons of imperialism, but rather of pragmatism: the 7,000 kilometers of Russo-Kazakh border, in the heart of the steppes, are nearly impossible to secure, and necessitate that the clandestine flows be controlled downstream, therefore consolidating Central Asia's role as a buffer zone for Russia. During Vladimir Putin's two mandates (2000-08) and despite the withdrawal of the Russian troops from the external borders of the former Soviet Union, Moscow has succeeded in regaining its status as the Central Asian states' number one strategic partner. It has set up several multilateral structures and signed many bilateral treaties and agreements in all military domains, from joint exercises and personnel training to the renting of facilities and the sale of arms.

THE MULTILATERAL FRAMEWORK AND ITS LIMITS

Three regional organizations supervise, with various degrees of efficiency, the military relations between Russia and Central Asia: the CIS, the Collective Security Treaty Organization (CSTO), and the Shanghai Cooperation Organization (SCO).

While the CIS member states have signed numerous military cooperation agreements, the Community has not proven to be viable in strategic terms, given the divergence in the political and geopolitical directions of its members. During the Tajik civil war, a CIS collective of peacekeeping forces was deployed in the country; it was comprised of Russia's 201st Motor

Rifle Division and a battalion each from Kazakhstan, Kyrgyzstan, and Uzbekistan.[12] For the Central Asian region, one of the real, practical realizations of the CIS multilateral security cooperation was the creation of the Joint Air Defense System, the main functions of which were to coordinate the Central Asian airspace defense with Russia. Moreover, each year since the early 1990s, Russia has held joint military exercises with some of the CIS members at the Ashuluk training base in the Astrakhan region. In 2009, these exercises, which simulate terrorist attacks in the Caucasus and Central Asia, have been the most important since the creation of the CIS.[13]

Of the numerous CIS institutions, only the Anti-Terrorist Center (ATC) and the Council of Border Guard Agency Commanders are, properly speaking, functional. In December 2000, Russia, Kazakhstan, Kyrgyzstan, and Tajikistan agreed on a proposal made by the CIS Council of Defense Ministers to create an anti-terrorist center based in Moscow.[14] Half of the Center is financed by Russia alone, the other half being evenly distributed among the other member states. It provides the Central Asian security services with training and offers annual anti-terrorist exercises called South Anti-Terror, administered by the FSB Center of Special Actions. Numerous Kyrgyz, Kazakh, and Tajik officers and customs officials have gone there for training. In 2008, 69 Kazakhstani officers, 128 Kyrgyz, and 145 Tajiks were trained in the FSB border guard services, whereas 15 Tajiks were sent to the Ukraine, and 30 Tajiks and 29 Kyrgyz to Kazakhstan. It seems that since 2005 and 2006, Uzbekistan and Turkmenistan have both been asking for cooperation from the Russian FSB. The Center includes a Central Asian section based in Bishkek and manages an anti-terrorist database.

Another institution is the CIS Council of Border Guard Agency Commanders, which organizes regular cooperation between Russian and Central Asian services. It is trying to influence the legislative documents adopted on the question of security at the borders — in particular, more recently, concerning the flows of illegal migrants — and to obstruct the North Atlantic Treaty Organization's (NATO) presence in the region. It has its own network of information exchange and finances its professional training, as well as technical collaboration between services, in Russia.[15] In 2009, the Council organized Exercise Rubezh Otechestva 2009, which simulated actions against arms, drugs, and migrant-trafficking networks at the Afghan-Central Asian borders.[16] It has also organized operations to fight against poaching in the Caspian Sea. Utilizing former Soviet structures, the Council is able to coordinate seminars several times per year and maintains close contacts between institutions, thanks to human connections, the shared knowledge of Russian, and also charitable programs for the customs service officers (support for veterans, etc.). At the end of 2008, the Council signed a cooperation program with the Regional Anti-Terrorist Structure (RATS) of the SCO based in Tashkent, but it does not appear to have led to any common operations.

Russian-Central Asian multilateral military collaborations are mainly geared toward the CSTO, which includes Russia and the Central Asian states (excepting Turkmenistan, Byelorussia, and Armenia.) The CSTO regularly reunites the Foreign Ministers, Defense Ministers, and Secretaries of Security Councils of member states.[17] A permanent body of the CSTO and the Council of Defense Ministers are responsible for planning and executing decisions on military matters.[18] The

CSTO makes provision for the sale of military material to member countries at Russian domestic market prices, which is of great interest to the Central Asian states, whose military budgets increased on average by 50 percent in 2007, and probably by as much again in 2008.[19] Equipment for border control (light artillery, night-vision devices, camouflage, radio devices, all terrain vehicles, etc.) is highly prized. Since 2005, the CSTO has also revived cooperation between the Russian and Central Asian military industrial complexes. The Intergovernmental Committee for Military and Economic Cooperation (ICMEC) is pushing for closer integration of the national military industries.[20] In this framework, Kazakhstan has provided 45 training slots for Kyrgyz military personnel, and Byelorussia has also offered to host Central Asian officers. Officer exchanges between 45 Russian, 6 Byelorussian, 3 Kazakh, 1 Kyrgyz, 1 Tajik, and 1 Armenian military academies have also taken place.[21]

CSTO common military exercises are carried out annually in one of the member countries. They simulate terrorist attacks (called *Rubezh*) or anti-narcotics operations (*Kanal*), and permit greater interaction between border guards and other police and military units. New operations were organized along similar lines: Arsenal against arms trafficking, *Nelegal* against illegal immigration, and *Proxi* against technological criminality.[22] Operation KANAL is alleged to have resulted in the seizure of more than 300 tons of drugs and illicit substances in 2008 alone, and has reportedly become a permanent institution.[23] The same year, the creation of a Coordination Council for the fight against clandestine immigration shows that this question, relatively neglected to date, has become one of the new obsessions of the border services. In the CSTO

11

framework, the Collective Rapid Deployment Force (CRDF) for Central Asia, comprising about 4,000 persons made up of Kazakh, Kyrgyz, Russian, and Tajik units, is the only trained armed force capable of rapidly intervening. It aims mainly at border securitization in case of violation by terrorist groups.[24] The permanent operational group of the general staff is based in Bishkek. In 2009, a decision was made to upgrade the force to about 15,000 men. Each state will establish its own permanent battalion, which it will station on its own territory, but which can also be called upon to lead joint operations in one of the member states at any time.[25] Uzbekistan has stated that it will only participate in the CRDF on a case-by-case basis, while Byelorussia postponed signing the agreement until October 2009.

The SCO, despite its security rhetoric, is relatively inactive in practice and unable to compete with Russia.[26] It has helped to defuse a number of potential conflicts between China and the former Soviet states, especially the border disputes, but has not yet succeeded in organizing multilateral peace operations inside or outside of its own area.[27] Since it was not designed to become a supranational organization whose members have reduced sovereignty, it does not have a defined military structure like the CSTO. It is not a military defense alliance like NATO, nor is it concerned with creating multilateral military or police units. Despite the 2004 establishment of the Regional Anti-Terrorist Structure, meant to develop common approaches to combat terrorist movements, any multilateral security dynamic remains embryonic.[28] Even so, this makes it possible to engage in information exchange and doctrinal dialogue, which facilitates better understanding between security structures. The SCO seems primarily to be a reflection of Chinese willingness to support what Beijing has called a "healthy Central Asian order," free from any separatist, Islamist, or pro-Western forces that might act to destabilize China.

Since 2005, the SCO has led exercises called Peace Missions, which feature large-scale combat operations and, at least in theory, bring together the totality of members. In August 2007, the *Rubezh* exercises of the CSTO were associated with the SCO Peace Mission in the Chelyabinsk region under the orders of a commandment structure based at Urumqi for the occasion. This joint exercise gathered more than 4,000 men, including 2,000 Russians and 1,700 Chinese.[29] In 2009, the peace mission was focused on naval exercises, probably in view of a Taiwan or North Korean scenario.[30] However, despite this cooperation, military relations between member states remain complex. Russia has refused to participate in several exercises in which China has taken part and has seemed less committed to promoting the military aspect of the SCO. Moscow favors giving priority to the CSTO, and wants to maintain its military monopoly over Central Asia, rather than share security responsibilities with Beijing. Moreover, neither Russia nor China is inclined to disclose sensitive information about new technologies or their respective nuclear complexes.

The SCO therefore does not play a major role in Russia's multilateral involvement in Central Asia; Moscow has many other vectors of leverage and is not really interested in cooperating closely with China. The CIS Anti-Terrorist Center and the Council of Border Guard Agencies demonstrate that although the classical army corps, under the control of the Defense Ministries, are not very cooperative within the CIS, the special sections attached to the Ministries of the Interior and Emergency Situations and secret services are still linked by their Soviet past and continue to work together. Apart from its role in the elaboration of collective strategies against terrorism, transnational dangers, and drug-trafficking, the CSTO is the only regional institution with a genuine military dimension. Through the CSTO, Moscow hopes to weaken the American military partnership in the region and to make itself into the necessary intermediary of military relations between the West and the Central Asian regimes.[31] The Kremlin, for instance, has asked that the CSTO be considered on par with NATO, which would enable it to talk on equal terms with the latter and force the Central Asian regimes to go through Moscow before engaging in any joint military initiative with the West.

Moscow is quite clear-sighted about the fact that the Central Asian regimes do not favor intra-Central Asian collaborations: the Russian elites have a good memory of the internal conflicts among the republics during Soviet times and did not set their hopes, as did Western countries in the 1990s, on some form of Central Asian union. Central Asian military cooperation is, in fact, practically at a standstill and only operates in more general frameworks involving neighboring powers such as Russia and China, or else Western countries, such as NATO's Partnership for Peace and the EU Border Management Programme for Central Asia, chiefly financed by the EU and implemented by the UN Development Programme. The Central Asian Economic Community, founded in 1994 by Kazakhstan, Kyrgyzstan, and Uzbekistan, had created a tripartite battalion, the *Centrazbat*, formed to coordinate joint military exercises and to be deployed outside the

Central Asian zone as a peacekeeping force under the auspices of the UN, but the project has been stopped. In 2002-03, the region's two weakest states, which are also the most under threat from transnational dangers, namely Kyrgyzstan and Tajikistan, reached an understanding on two agreements involving military cooperation, one between the border guards and the military units stationed at their joint borders, and another between their respective Defense Ministries and security agencies. This reinforcement of Kyrgyz-Tajik cooperation was confirmed in 2007, when Presidents Kurmanbek Bakiev and Emomali Rakhmon met to specify the nature of the cooperation between their respective security services and to discuss the implementation of measures for the securitization of the mountainous cross-border spaces.[32] Despite this attempt at agreement, the Central Asian states have not really succeeded in developing a consequential military cooperation, and only collaborate in the framework of larger structures involving other partners.

In view of the development differentials between the Central Asian countries and the various policies pursued by the regimes, the Kremlin has been compelled to consider each state on its own specific terms and to adopt a more differentiated policy. Moscow conceives Kazakhstan, its closest military and political ally in the Central Asian region, as a strategic partner in post-Soviet space, and has no other choice than to accept its decisionmaking autonomy and multivector foreign policy. Tajikistan and Kyrgyzstan, for their part, are perceived as beneficiaries of Russian military aid: they are seen more as burdens to bear and destabilizing factors to be controlled than as equal partners. Moreover, the negotiations over the hiring of the bases at Manas, Kyrgyzstan, and at Aini, Tajikistan, are complicated: the Kyrgyz and Tajik governments see them as a unique financial opportunity, which they exploit for all it is worth. The political tensions are also often transferred onto the military cooperation, for example, such as that between Moscow and Dushanbe at the end of 2009. Uzbekistan and Turkmenistan, on the other hand, are viewed as difficult-to-control countries: Russia sought to make the most of their geopolitical reorientation between 2003 and 2008, and was quite aware that their more or less pro-Russian policies were by no means assured for the long-term — should the chance arise, some anti-Russian policy may well be swiftly implemented, and this seems to have taken place since 2009. Bilateralism therefore dominates in the security domain as it allows more room for maneuver when protecting national interests of each state.

BILATERALISM, A MUCH MORE EFFECTIVE FRAMEWORK

Joint Exercises and Provision of Military Equipment.

From the beginning of the 1990s, Russia was clear about what it saw as the main concern for bilateral cooperation: the protection of the international borders of the former Soviet Union. Although Russian troops today are no longer in Kyrgyzstan, Turkmenistan, or Tajikistan, the FSB border service still conducts bilateral consultations on the securitization of borders in Kyrgyzstan and Tajikistan. Russian troops, who helped both countries create their own air defense systems in the 1990s, also train their air force personnel. Bilateral military exercises are regularly organized with Kazakhstan, Kyrgyzstan, and Tajikistan, focussed on drug-trafficking and illegal migrations, such as those, for instance, that Moscow and Astana undertook on the Caspian Sea in 2006.[33] Between 2009 and 2011, regular Russian-Kazakh exercises will take place annually.[34] After its geopolitical reversal in 2005, when it expelled the United States from the base at Karshi-Khanabad, Tashkent committed itself more clearly in favor of military cooperation with Moscow.[35] Some joint anti-terrorist exercises between Uzbekistan and Russia were organized in the military testing ground at Forish, the most sophisticated of the Uzbek military sectors. Built in 2000, it is situated on the heights of Mount Nuratau, at an altitude of more than 2,000 meters, and hosts a modern informatized system as well as a training firing range.[36] Members of the Russian special section Alfa reportedly also participated in the training of personnel from the Uzbek special services, which afterwards completed preparation in Moscow's FSB Center of Special Actions.[37] No joint exercises have been organized with the Turkmen army.

In the 1990s, the Russian industrial-military complex's lack of budget, not to mention that of the young Central Asian states, slowed military technological cooperation. However, since the start of the 2000s, *Rosobornoexport* has again been supplying the Central Asian states with large quantities of military equipment. Sometimes Russia offers the material in return for the rental of sites, mainly in Kyrgyzstan and Tajikistan, or else it sells it at preferential prices, at least to Kazakhstan, Uzbekistan, and Turkmenistan, which are the only Central Asian states able to finance their armies. Thanks to several agreements signed between Astana and Moscow, Russia has become Kazakhstan's primary supplier of defense equipment, tanks, helicopters, planes, spare parts, and weapons.[38] Kazakhstan is the first client of the Kazan helicopter factory, and several small and medium tonnage ships are going to be constructed in the Tartar factories of the Russian industrial-military complex, at Kazakh request.[39] Astana, in addition, also conceives itself as a future supplier of arms to the other Central Asian states in the medium term.[40]

The Russian Ministry of Defense has regularly signed agreements with Kyrgyzstan and Tajikistan for the provision of free military aid. In 2005, Russia and Uzbekistan signed a major strategic cooperation agreement according to which Moscow has committed to support the Uzbek regime in case of upheavals, and to supply Tashkent with diverse categories of crowd dispersing equipment. In exchange, Uzbekistan was supposed to grant Russian troops access to 10 airports and to open a military base for them on the national territory, which has not materialized. Even if the relations between Ashgabat and Moscow are riddled with suspicion, sometimes conflict-ridden, negotiations in strategic sectors such as arms sales have always been carried out parallel with official diplomatic relations. As of 1997, Russian-Turkmen military cooperation practically ground to a halt. However, since 2003, *Rosoboronexport* has revived contacts with the Turkmen authorities, in particular, in technical assistance for the aviation and arms sales sectors. In 2009, Ashgabat ordered 10 T-90 tanks from the Uralvagonzavod factory, following its purchase of the heavy multiple rocket launcher, Smerch, and signed several contracts for the renovation of Soviet material.[41] Russia therefore largely equips the Central Asian armies with infantry weapons, ammunition, night-vision apparatuses, as well as planes, helicopters, anti-missile defense systems, and tanks, and also provides after-sales service and repairs.

Personnel Training.

The second largest domain of cooperation, which assures Russia its supremacy in the military sector, is personnel training. The Soviet legacy in this sector has enabled Moscow to help train a majority of Central Asian military personnel.[42] The training is offered at two levels: for young, enlisted soldiers who receive all their higher education in Russia (from 3 to 5 years, depending of the degree to be attained) as well as for officers requiring refresher courses or more targeted, specialized training. Several hundred high-level Central Asians have earned their diplomas at Russian military academies, which serve as models for the Central Asian military schools. Kazakh military training establishments have, for instance, been remodeled along Russian lines. Finally, the two Russian military bases in Kyrgyzstan and Tajikistan also offer specialized on-site training. Several tens of Russian instructors work for the Tajik army on a contractual basis, and Russian military advisors supervise the training of personnel within the Military Institute of the Ministry of Defense.

In the framework of the 1992 Russian-Kazakh treaty of cooperation and assistance and the military cooperation agreement signed between the two countries in 1994, Russia has committed to training at least 500 Kazakh officers in its military academies each year. Between 1993 and 2006, about 2,500 Kazakh military personnel were fully trained in the institutes of the Russian Defense Ministry, while about 15,000 received some courses or training.[43] In 2006, more than 800 Kazakh military personnel were distributed throughout about 40 Russian establishments, with Kazakhstan alone representing about one-third of the military personnel from the CIS trained in Russia. In Kyrgyzstan, training also constitutes a crucial sector of Russian military aid: more than 800 persons have reportedly been trained between 1992 and 2007.[44] In 2008, Kyrgyz Defense Minister Ismail Isakov acknowledged that about 90 percent of the Kyrgyz army officers trained abroad were trained in Russia.[45] For this same year, 260 student officers out of the 300 in training were placed in Russia and benefited from an education that Moscow covered completely at the financial level.

The situation is similar in Tajikistan: between 2002 and 2007, Moscow provided complementary training to approximately 500 Tajik officers.[46] Since the bilateral agreement of 1994, Dushanbe has sent between 300 and 400 persons to be trained in Russian military institutions each year. Several tens of young specialists are going to be trained at the Russian military base. Russia also contributes to the training of elite Tajik troops, in particular the First Brigade of Special Operations. Close to 70 percent of the officers of this armed corps graduated from Russian military institutes, in particular from the parachuting school of Ryazan and the schools of the Interior Ministry in Perm and Saint-Petersburg. The Russian-Tajik military cooperation treaty gave birth to the FSB Operational Border Guard Group, which works with the Tajik border guards, trains specialists, and offers its technological assistance. For geopolitical reasons, Russian-Uzbek cooperation in the domain of training cadres remained particularly weak throughout the 1990s. Since Tashkent's geopolitical turnabout in favor of Moscow, Russian-

Uzbek cooperation has accelerated. Between 2001 and 2006, close to 250 Uzbek officers were trained in Russia, of which 70 received all their higher education in the establishments of the Russian Defense Ministry.[47] As for Turkmenistan, it appears that some of its officers have also been being trained in Russia, but no figures are available.

Russian Military Facilities in Central Asia.

The Russian authorities have succeeded in retaining or in reacquiring a number of military and research facilities in Kazakhstan, Kyrgyzstan, and Tajikistan.[48] The most important ones from the entire former Soviet Union are those in Kazakhstan, which constitute a major element of the Russian defense system. Russia has no military base there, properly speaking, but since the 1990s, Astana, Kazakhstan's capital city, has given Moscow the use of several firing ranges in exchange for military material, specialized maintenance, and officer training.[49] Russia, for instance, rents the famous Baikonur Cosmodrome from Astana (70 percent of Russian rocket launches start there). A new agreement signed in 2004 extends the hiring of the site until 2050. As of 2008, the cosmodrome, which hosts close to 3,000 specialists, is no longer under the responsibility of the Russian Defense Ministry but under that of a civil institution, the Federal Space Agency of Russia, Roskosmos. In association with Baikonur, Russia has an evacuation site for space debris near Karaganda. Russia also rents weapons and missile launch centers in the regions of Atyrau and western Kazakhstan, as well as ballistic missile test firing ranges and training firings in the regions of Karaganda, Zhambul, Aktobe, and Kzyl-Orda, and the Gulchad site, close to Priozersk, in the region of Lake Balkhash, which monitors ballistic missiles and space objects circulating above Asia as far as 3,000 km away.[50]

In Kyrgyzstan, Russia has the Kant base (about 20 km from Bishkek, at Manas airport) at its disposal. Opened in 2003, it can accommodate close to 800 men, along with large ground-attack aircraft and army helicopters.[51] The Kant aerodrome was built in 1941 for the purpose of hosting the Odessa pilot school, and then displaced by the advance of Nazi troops into Soviet territory. In 1956, the school was transformed into a training establishment for cadres of Soviet aviation and that of "brother countries." The base, which belongs to the Volga military district, today hosts part of the Collective Rapid Deployment Force and supports the Russian presence in neighboring Tajikistan.[52] Moscow plans to increase its military presence in Kyrgyzstan at the Kant air base, but also, maybe, by opening a new base in the south, near Osh. First put forward in 2005, and again in spring 2009 with the support of Bishkek, this very controversial idea elicited virulent critiques from Tashkent, which claimed it was being directly targeted.[53] Russia controls several other Kyrgyz sites, including both the seismic control station of the Russian Defense Ministry in the Tian Shan mountain range, which monitors nuclear weapons trial activities in China and South Asia, and the Kara-Balta station at Chaldovar in the Chui region, which depends on the Russian military fleet and communicates with submarines and surface ships patrolling in the Pacific and Indian Oceans. Russia also has a presence close to Karakol, at the Koi-Sary military base near the Issyk-Kul Lake. This site, which is often called the underwater Baikonur, has today begun to emerge from the military secrecy that has surrounded it until now, to the extent that Rosoboronexport has even raised the possibility of holding an international weapons exhibition there.[54]

Since the signing of a 2004 treaty with Dushanbe, Tajikistan is now host to Moscow's largest military base outside the Federation's borders. The negotiations over the transformation of the 201st division into a permanent Russian military base started in 1999 but closed in 2004. The Tajik authorities would like Moscow to pay rent for the base—something the Kremlin has always refused to do—instead offering material advantages, such as, for example, arms sales to the Tajik Army at domestic Russian prices, and training of Tajik military personnel. The former 201st armed Division, now a member of the Rapid Collective Deployment Force, is stationed in Dushanbe, while motor rifle regiments and tanks are distributed between Kurgan-Tiube and Kuliab. Russia has also been allowed to occupy the Aini air base close to Dushanbe, which stations Russian helicopter squadrons, and the Okno spatial surveillance center, located at an altitude of 2,200 meters, close to the Chinese border near Nurek.[55] Built at the end of the 1970s, Okno, which only became totally operational in 2002, hosts an optical and electronic monitoring station for the Russian space forces and can see as far as 40,000 km away, thanks to the exceptional visibility provided by local climatic conditions. It also has an anti-missile warning system able to monitor nearly all of Eurasian airspace. The specialists who work there are all Russian citizens and generally hold their posts for about 10 years. Russia does not have any military facilities in either Turkmenistan or Uzbekistan.

The Relaunch of the Central Asia Military-Industrial Complex.

With the collapse of the Soviet Union, all the Central Asian firms linked to the military-industrial complex almost shut down. Since 2005, Moscow's influence, bolstered by the importance of its Soviet legacy, has further been enhanced by the re-launching of the Central Asia military-industrial complex, but without either Turkmenistan — Ashgabat is not interested in such cooperation — or Tajikistan — the only Central Asian country to inherit practically no equipment from the Soviet Army. In the three other countries, Moscow and the local governments have a shared interest in preserving the skills of their companies, and in reviving these facilities for joint export to third world countries. Indeed, many of the military items produced in Central Asia have real export potential, especially to China and India.

In Kazakhstan, five Russian-Kazakh joint ventures now work in various military sectors: anti-air defense systems (Granit JV), torpedo construction (Kirov mechanical engineering works), anti-ship mines (ZIK-STO JV), communications equipment (Kirov factory), naval materiel, and spare parts for torpedoes (Zenit, in Uralsk).[56] Joint space activities have broadened in scope since the launching of the Baiterek Space Rocket Complex, which will confirm the emergence of a specifically Kazakh space industry, although its specialists were all educated in Russia in the framework of the strategic partnership between the two countries. Kyrgyzstan also hopes to revitalize its joint military ventures with the support of Rosoboronexport, which opened an office in Bishkek. The Dastan JV continues to produce rocket torpedo and electronic systems used by the Russian navy,[57] the Ainur JV and Bishkek Stamping Works manufactures cartridge cases for infantry weapons, and the Zhanar JV is specialized in border protection equipment. New types of torpedoes are produced by the Ozero JV, formerly the Dagdizel production factory, which moved to Dagestan near Karakul in 1943 and today is 95 percent Russian-owned. During the Soviet period, the factory produced up to 1,000 torpedoes per year, which were tested in the depths of Issyk-Kul Lake and then transported to Russia via a railway connecting Issyk-Kul to Almaty.

Uzbekistan has also tried to revive its cooperation with Russia in the aeronautical domain. The Chkalov factory, called TAPO, is famous for its production of large military Il-76 transporters (even though it also has charge of several productions of less importance, such as the small Il-114 planes and the wings of the An-70 military planes). The factory has experienced several setbacks since the fall of the Union of Soviet Socialist Republics (USSR). Whereas close to a thousand military transport planes were built there during the Soviet period, only 10 new units bound for the Indian military have been produced since independence. Tensions between TAPO and Ilyushin over the delivery of the famous Il-76 (90 percent made in Russia but completely assembled in Tashkent) destined for the Chinese army hit a peak in 2006, before they were in part resolved by the cession of 50 percent of the shares of TAPO to the Russian United Aircraft Corporation, which gathers the main Russian constructors (Mig, Sukhoi, Ilyushin, and Tupolev).[58]

The stakes are important for the Russian military-industrial complex: Tashkent remains the only area of the former Soviet Union where the fourth-generation Il-76 MF are constructed to Western environmental standards, whereas Russia only possesses older generations, nearly all of which are prohibited for overflight in European airspace. For Rosoboronexport, the Tashkent factory must, above all, meet the export orders, while the Ulyanovsk factory is reserved for the needs of the Russian military-industrial complex. The strategic partnership agreement signed in 2004 also makes provision for cooperation in the spatial sector: Roskosmos hopes to gain access to the Maidanak observatory, which is situated on the Suffa Plateau between Tashkent and Samarcande. The site's modernization, to be carried out with Russian financing, was confirmed by a bilateral agreement signed in 2008.[59] In 2007, a new Russian-Uzbek joint venture UzRosAvia was created to provide for the repairs on Russian military helicopters at the Chirchik factory close to Tashkent.[60] The same year, a decision was also made enabling Uzbekistan to have some of its Soviet planes and helicopters repaired in Russian factories, in exchange for which Moscow is able to use the Ustyurt Plateau to conduct spatial tests, but the project appears not to have come to fruition.[61]

CONCLUSION

In the 1990s, Russia's military presence in Central Asian revolves mainly around its control over the southern borders of the former Soviet Union. Throughout this decade, Russia had practically no interest in other military sectors, with the obvious exception of the rental of the Baikonur Cosmodrome, and found itself competing with new partners such as NATO, which set up cooperation procedures in areas in which Russia showed little interest. In the 2000s, following the opening of American bases in the region, Russia's geopolitical revival, the rapprochement between Putin and the Central Asian regimes and the re-launching of the industrial-military complex enabled Moscow to regain power. Russia left aside the question of border management—a Soviet legacy—to invest in dynamic sectors such as the sale of military material and the training of Central Asian army officers. The Kremlin promotes many arguments: the power of a military-industrial complex able to sell material at particularly low, affordable prices for Central Asian budgets; Russian global economic involvement in the region, which makes it possible for Moscow to negotiate, in the same stroke, economic, political, and military cooperation, as was shown in discussions with Bishkek in February 2009; and, above all, training structures, which are attractive to Central Asian military cadres, since in them not only do they find a common language, namely Russian, but also Soviet traditions with which they are familiar.

However, we can question Russia's capacity to apprehend the future threats likely to affect Central Asia. For the moment, Moscow is living on its Soviet cultural heritage, which enables it to appear as the most obvious choice of partner, in particular at levels of language and training. However, while they all share intelligence information, the Central Asian armies and security services are distrustful of their Russian colleagues, and even Kazakhstan has tried to gain autonomy from the coercion of the Russian SVR by creating the Syrbar agency in the spring of 2009. Indeed, some sections of the Russian security services established in Central Asia are regularly accused of playing with fire by supplying clandestine groups or fuelling underlying conflicts between the states. The lack of analytical capacity inside Russian military structures also raises problems for elaborating strategies vis-à-vis Central Asia, but the Central Asian security services themselves are badly prepared in terms of competence-building. Dangers continue to be interpreted foremost in military terms, whereas the major risks include asymmetrical wars linked to the Afghan neighbor (drug trafficking), possible internal destabilization (Islamism, popular movements, etc.), or managing the risks of natural catastrophes. The Russian army itself faces significant challenges concerning its own modernization, which thus far it has been unable to meet. It will therefore be difficult for Russia to offer the Central Asian states anything more than a conventional and partly outdated conception of the strategic stakes of the 21st century. Finally, the partnership with Moscow will do nothing to facilitate the elaboration of a comprehensive security service reform in Central Asia, the underlying idea of which is that security must be effective, accountable, and indivisible.[62]

ENDNOTES - CHAPTER 1

1. M. Laruelle, S. Peyrouse, "The Militarization of the Caspian Sea: 'Great Games' and 'Small Games' Over the Caspian Fleets," *The China and Eurasia Forum Quarterly*, Vol. 7, No. 2, 2009, pp. 17-35.

2. M. Pikulina, *Uzbekistan in the Mirror of Military Security. An Historical Preface to Current Events*, Central Asia Series, Camberley, Surrey, UK: Defence Academy of the United Kingdom, 1999; O. Sidorov, "Vooruzhennye sily Kazakhstana — vchera i segodnia," *Centrasia.ru*, March 27, 2007, available from *www.centrasia. ru/newsA.php?st=1174025820*.

3. *Istoriia 201-I Gachinskoi dvazhdy Krasnoznamennoi MSD*, Russian Ministry of Defense, 2005, available from *www.mil.ru/848/104 5/1272/17521/19356/19385/index.shtml*.

4. M. Makhonina, *Voenno-politicheskoe Sotrudnichestvo Mezhdu Rossiei i Tadzhikistanom 1993-1999*, Dushanbe, Tajikistan: Akademiya Nauk, 1999.

5. *Ibid.*

6. O. Sidorov, "Vooruzhennye sily Tadzhikistana—vchera i segodnia," *War and Peace.ru*, March 14, 2007, available from *www.warandpeace.ru/ru/analysis/vprint/9351/*.

7. Z. K. Suerkulov, "Kyrgyzskaya Respublika v Central'no-Aziatskom Regione: Nekotorye Voprosy Bezopasnosti," *Voennaya Mysl'*, No. 8, 2006, pp. 58-63.

8. A. P. Yarkov, *Kazaki v Kyrgyzstane*, Bishkek, Kyrgyzstan: KRSU, 2002.

9. More information can be found in M. Laruelle and S. Peyrouse, *China as a Neighbor. Central Asian Perspectives and Strategies*, Washington, DC: Central Asia and Caucasus Institute, 2009.

10. G. Mikhailov, "Na Parad—Amerikanskii Kamuflizh, na Sluzhby—Rossiiskii," *Nezavisimaya Gazeta*, January 21, 2008, available from *www.ng.ru/courier/2008-01-21/17_kamufliazh.html*.

11. A. Korbut, "Trudovaya Armiya Poka Ostaetsia," *VPK News*, September 2007, available from *www.vpk-news.ru/article.asp?pr_sign=archive.2007.202.articles.cis_02*; "Turkmeniya Namerena Razvivat' Svoiu Armiiu," *Cry. Ru*, September 5, 2007, available from *www.cry.ru/2007/09/05/articles*.

12. V. Paramonov, O. Stopolski, *Russia and Central Asia: Multilateral Security Cooperation*, Central Asia Series, Camberley, Surrey, UK: Defence Academy of the United Kingdom, 2008, pp. 2-3.

13. V. Mukhin, "Koalitsionnye Ucheniya v Ashukule Priznany Uspeshnymi," *Novoye Voennoe Obozrenye—Nezavisimaya Gazeta*, September 1, 2009, available from *nvo.ng.ru/forces/2000-09-01/3_ashuluk.html*.

14. See its web site, *www.atcsng.ru*.

15. See its web site, *www.skpw.ru/*.

16. "Po Initsiative Pogranichnykh Vedomstv Kazakhstana, Kyrgyzstana, Rossii, Tadzhikistana i Uzbekistana v Kurgans-koi Oblasti Provedena Sovmestnaya Spetsial'naia Pogranitch-naia Operatsiya 'Rubezhi Otechestva 2009'," *Federal'naya Sluzhba Migratsii*, October 7, 2009, available from *www.fms.gov.ru/press/ news/news_detail.php?ID=30881*.

17. See its web site, *www.dkb.gov.ru/*.

18. A. Nikitin, "Post-Soviet Military-Political Integration: The Collective Security Treaty Organization and its Relations with the EU and NATO," *The China and Eurasia Forum Quarterly*, Vol. 5, No. 1, 2007, p. 35-44.

19. "Tsentral'naya Aziya Gotovitsia k Oborone. Voennye Raskhody Postsovetskikh Stran Regiona Uvelichilis' v 2007 g. na Polovinu," *Ferghana.ru*, January 23, 2007, available from *www. ferghana.ru/article.php?id=4859*.

20. "ODKB Voyenno-Tekhnicheskoe sotrudnichestvo," available from *www.dkb.gov.ru/start/index.htm*.

21. See *www.dkb.gov.ru/start/index.htm*.

22. "Problemy Sotrudnichestva ODKB i SHOS v Oblasti Bezopasnosti," *East Time*, July 3, 2009, available from *www. easttime.ru/reganalitic/1/212p.html*.

23. "Spetsoperatsiya ODKB 'Kanal' Poluchila Status Postoy-anno Deistvuiuchshego Proekta," *Novosti Belarusi*, June 5, 2009, available from *www.interfax.by/news/belarus/56181*.

24. "Nikolai Bordyuzha: Formirovanie KSOR Prodolzhaet-sya," *Soyuz*, October 29, 2009, available from *www.soyuz.by/ ru/?guid=70892*.

25. V. Socor, "CSTO Summit: Rapid Deployment Forces Advance at a Snail's Pace," *Eurasia Daily Monitor*, Vol. 6, No. 24, February 5, 2009, available from *Category: Eurasia Daily Monitor, Vlad's Corner, Military/Security, Russia, Central Asia www. jamestown.org/single/?no_cache=1&tx_ttnews%5Btt_news%5D =34460*.

26. Its members are Russia, China, the four Central Asian states with the exception of Turkmenistan, and observer status has been acquired by India, Pakistan, Iran, and Mongolia.

27. A. Iwashita, "The Shanghai Cooperation Organization and Its Implications for Eurasian Security: A New Dimension of 'Partnership' after the post-Cold War Period," *Slavic Eurasia's Integration into the World Economy and Community*, Asahikawa, Japan: Slavic Research Center, Hokkaido University, 2004, pp. 259-281; A. J. K. Bailes, P. Dunay, P. Guang, and M. Troitskiy, *The Shanghai Cooperation Organization,* SIPRI Policy Paper No. 17, Stockholm, Sweden: Stockholm International Peace Research Institute, May 2007.

28. Zh. Huasheng, *Kitai, Tsentral'naya Aziya i Shankhaiskaya Organizatsiya Sotrudnichestva*, Working Paper No. 5, Moscow, Russia: Carnegie Endowment for International Peace, 2005.

29. R. N. McDermott, "The Rising Dragon. SCO Peace Mission 2007," *Jamestown Occasional Paper*, Washington, DC: Jamestown Foundation, October 2007.

30. S. Blank, "Peace-Mission 2009: A Military Scenario Beyond Central Asia," *China Brief*, Vol. 9, No. 17, August 20, 2009, available from *www.jamestown.org/programs/chinabrief/single/?tx_ttnews%5Btt_news%5D=35433&tx_ttnews%5BbackPid%5D=25&cHash=201d76e87b.*

31. A. Frost, "The Collective Security Treaty Organization, the Shanghai Cooperation Organization, and Russia's Strategic Goals in Central Asia," *The China and Eurasia Forum Quarterly*, Vol. 7, No. 3, 2009, pp. 83-102.

32. "V Bishkeke Sostoialis' Peregovory Prezidentov Kyrgyzstana i Tadzhikistana," *CentrAsia*, September 18, 2007, available from *www.centrasia.ru/newsA.php?st=1190099040*; "Pogranichniki Kyrgyzstana i Tadzhikistan Obsudili Razrabotku Plana Vzaimnogo Sotrudnichestva," *The Review of Central Asia*, June 21, 2007, available from *www.c-asia.org/post/index.php?year=2007&today=21&month=6.*

33. "V Kaspiiskom More Proidut Sovmestnye Rossiisko-Kazaxstanskie Ucheniya," *News Rin.ru*, June 19, 2006, available from *news.rin.ru/news/72924/2/*.

34. "Rossiisko-Kazaxstankie Voennye Ucheniya Stanut Yezhegodnym," *Altai Transgranichnyi*, October 7, 2008, available from *www.altaiinter.info/news/?id=19902*.

35. R. Burnashev and I. Chernykh, "Changes in Uzbekistan's Military Policy after the Andijan Events," *The China and Eurasia Forum Quarterly*, Vol. 5, No. 1, 2007, pp. 67-73.

36. R. Streshnev, "Forish—Proverka Boem," *Krasnaya Zvezda*, September 24, 2005, available from *www.redstar.ru/2005/09/24_09/1_01.html*.

37. "Antiterroristicheskii Tsentr' SNG," *Anti-terror*, available from *anti-teror.ucoz.ua/index/0-29*.

38. "Rosoboroneksport Ozhidaet Zakaz iz Kazakhstana na Boevye Mashiny Podderzhki Tankov Proizvodstva Uralvagonzavoda," *Nomad*, June 23, 2008, available from *www.nomad.su/?a=4-200806230818*.

39. M. Slavin, "Na Kaspii Postroit Novyi Flot?" ("Is a new fleet being constructed on the Caspian?"), *Sootechestvennik*, available from *www.russedina.ru/?id=5926*.

40. R. McDermott, "Kazakhstan kak Potentsialn'yi Postavchshik Oruzhiya," *Geokz.tv*, June 23, 2008, available from *www.geokz.tv/article.php?aid=5466*.

41. "Turkmenie Kupila Partiiu Rossiiskikh Tankov T-90," *Lenta.ru*, July 7, 2009, available from *lenta.ru/news/2009/07/08/tanks/*.

42. E. Marat, "Soviet Military Legacy and Regional Security Cooperation in Central Asia," *The China and Eurasia Forum Quarterly*, Vol. 5, No. 1, 2007, pp. 83-114.

43. Paramonov and Stopolski, *Russia and Central Asia*, p. 2.

44. *Ibid.*, p. 6.

45. "90% Ofitserov Armii Kirgizii Yavliaiutsia Vypusnika-mi Rossiiskiikh Vyzov," *Rosbalt*, March 26, 2008, available from www.rosbalt.ru/2008/03/26/468579.html.

46. Paramonov and Stopolski, *Russia and Central Asia*, p. 10.

47. *Ibid.*, p. 10.

48. Z. Lachowski, "Foreign Military Bases in Eurasia," SIPRI Policy Paper, No. 18, Stockholm, Sweden: Stockholm International Peace Research Institute, June 2007, pp. 43-61.

49. M. Kenzhetayev, "Russian-Kazakhstan Military and Technical Cooperation: Structure and Perceptive," *Export of Arms*, No. 5, 1998, available from *www.armscontrol.ru/atmtc/kazakhstan/article_mtc_kazakhstan.htm*.

50. "Vse Rossiiskii Bazy," *Vlast'*, No. 19 (723), May 21, 2007, available from *www.kommersant.ru/doc.aspx?DocsID=766827*.

51. L. Li, "Na Rossiiskoi Voyennoi Baze Kant Uvelichat Kolichestvo Boevykh Samoletov," *Regnum.ru*, April 20, 2009, available from *www.rg.ru/2009/04/20/sobkor-kant-anons.html*.

52. A. Yesenbekova, "Voennaya Bezopasnost' Kyrgyzstana i Sovremennyi Mir, ili Kak Svesti Kontsy s Konstami, *Cry.ry*, September 18, 2007, available from *http://www.cry.ru/2007/09/05/articles/204085/*.

53. E. Akhmadov, "Uzbekistan Concerned Over Russian Military Base in Ferghana," *Central Asia and Caucasus Analyst*, August 19, 2009, available from *www.cacianalyst.org/?q=node/5163*.

54. "Vse Rossiiskii Bazy," *Vlast'*.

55. V. Paramonov, O. Stolpovskii, "Dvukhstoronnee Sotrudnichestvo Rossii i Tadzhikistana v Voyennoi Sfere," *East Time*, December 11, 2008, available from *www.easttime.ru/analitic/1/2/536.html*.

56. Kazakhstan has its own program to develop a military-industrial complex, which it launched in 2007, see the site of

the Kazakh government available from *ru.government.kz/site/ news/2007/03/48.*

57. Russia has purchased 48 percent. Cf. "Kyrgyzstan: Prezident Bakiev Ratifitsiroval Soglasheniya po Rossiiskomu Kreditu," *Ferghana.ru*, February 10, 2009, available from *www.ferghana.ru/ news.php?id=11273&print=1.*

58. "TAPOiCH Voidet v Sostav OAK k Kontsu 2008 g.," *Vzgliad*, September 20, 2007, available from *vz.ru/news/2007/9/20/110855. html.*

59. "Rossiya i Uzbekistan Obsudili 'Kosmicheskie' Problem," *Bn.ru*, September 2, 2008, available from *www.bn.ru/ news/2008/09/02/36602.html.*

60. 'OAO Vertolety Rossii i OOO UzRosAviia Rzvivaiut Servisnoe Obsluzhivanie Rossiiskikh Vertoletov v Tsentral'no-Asiatskom Regione," *Arm-Tass*, December 7, 2009, available from *vpk.name/news/34377_oao_vertoletyi_rossii_i_ooo_uzrosavia_razvivayut_servisnoe_obsluzhivanie_rossiiskih_vertoletov_v_centralnoaziatskom_regione.html.*

61. "Uzbekistan i Rossiya Opredelyayut Perspektivy Sotrudnichesta v Voyennoi Sfere," *Interfax*, October 30, 2007. See more in Paramonov and Stopolski, "Dvukhstoronnee sotrudnichestvo Rossii i Uzbekistana v Voyennoi Sfere."

62. On SSR in each of the Central Asian countries, see M. Hartog, ed., *The SSR in Central Asia*, Groningen, The Netherlands: CESR, 2010. See also P. K. Forster, "International Factors Stopping Security Sector Reform: The Uzbek Case," *The China and Eurasia Forum Quarterly*, Vol. 5, No. 1, 2007, pp. 61-66.

CHAPTER 2

CONTEMPORARY ISSUES IN INTERNATIONAL SECURITY: CENTRAL ASIA

Dmitri Trenin

INTRODUCTION

Central Asia's five countries—Kazakhstan, Kyrgyzstan, Tajikistan, Turkmenistan, and Uzbekistan—are often lumped together. Outsiders, even most Russians who used to live in a common state with the Central Asians, find it difficult to differentiate among the five. Yet, the region is, in reality, five very distinct entities, which in some cases—e.g., Kyrgyzstan vs. Uzbekistan or Turkmenistan vs. the other four—have very little communication among themselves. The Central Asian Union, announced in the early 1990s, never managed to become a regional organization and ceased to exist in the 2000s. There is no obvious leader: Uzbekistan and Kazakhstan are the strongest two, but they form no duopoly, and the smaller three have little interest in accepting them as their mentors. It does not help that neither Tashkent nor Astana has any serious resources to spare for some common regional cause.[1] Thus, this chapter will mostly refer to Central Asia as a shorthand for its five new countries, without implying any particular unity among them.

Central Asia's five Soviet-era republics did not secede from the Soviet Union: it was the Union that imploded and abandoned them. The original version of the post-Soviet Commonwealth of Independent States (CIS) proclaimed on December 8, 1991, had no men-

35

tion of Central Asia. Even Kazakhstan was left out of the new project, and left to its own devices. This omission was repaired only on December 21, when, in an afterthought, 11 ex-Soviet leaders met in Almaty, Kazakhstan. Since then, to their credit, all five Central Asian states survived on their own, even though none of them had had any previous experience as a modern independent state. This is nothing but a small miracle. Also to their credit, they did not challenge one another's borders, even though those borders — initially internal administrative lines within the Union of Soviet Socialist Republics (USSR) — had been drawn arbitrarily, without due consideration of the ethnic distribution map of what used to be, 100 years ago, Russian Turkestan.

The authoritarian post-Soviet regimes of new Central Asian states have also largely survived, and some have already gone through transfers of power. Almost 2 decades after the collapse of the USSR, two of the most important countries, Kazakhstan and Uzbekistan, are still led by their founding presidents, Nursultan Nazarbayev and Islam Karimov. One, Turkmenistan, features a second-generation leader who had seamlessly succeeded Turkmenbashi, the Father of All Turkmens. Another one, Kyrgyzstan, comparatively more liberal under its first President, Askar Akayev, has gone through a color revolution of sorts, and continues to experience internal tensions. Finally, Tajikistan is ruled by Emomali Rakhmon, who emerged amidst a civil war that raged in 1992-93. However, that civil conflict, resulting in about 100,000 deaths and hundreds of thousands of refugees, is the only conflict to date in the former Soviet Union that has been successfully settled through a reconciliation accord, facilitated by Tehran and Moscow.

This relative calm does not mean that post-Soviet Central Asia has been an island of stability. The two biggest countries are yet to make their transition. Nazarbayev turned 70 in July 2010, and Karimov is 2 years older. Some local analysts compare their governing styles to Leonid Brezhnev's. The 2010s will most probably see new leaders in both Astana, Kazakhstan, and Tashkent, Uzbekistan. The passage will not be easy for Kazakhstan in view of inter-elite tensions there, and may be even rockier for Uzbekistan, which experienced radical Islamist raids in 1999-2000 and an uprising in Andijon in 2005. Turkmen President Gurbanguly Berdymuhamedov preempted his would-be rivals by moving with lightening speed to assume power after Saparmurat Niyazov's (i.e., Turkmenbashi's) sudden death in 2006, but he has continued the tradition of a one-man rule that totally depends on the state of health of the ruler. Kyrgyzstan, despite President Kurmanbek Bakiyev's efforts to establish a strong authority and curtail the powers of parliament and the rights of the opposition, has to cope with a growing gulf between the relatively more developed north and the rural south, which is the home of the local Islamist movement. Tajikistan has seen the opposition first integrated into a unity government, under a reconciliation accord, then stifled by Rakhmon, who made himself a president for life and is now formally addressed as "your majesty."

The absence of major territorial disputes has to be seen with a grain of salt. Kazakhstan's, Kyrgyzstan's, and Tajikistan's borders with China, which saw armed incidents in Soviet times, have been fixed. Nazarbayev has skillfully managed the issue of national and territorial integrity of Kazakhstan. By moving the capital from Almaty to Astana to the north, he secured the provinces adjacent to the Russian border. Not only do the ethnic Kazakhs now enjoy a majority in the country's overall population; there is no region anywhere in the country that has a non-Kazakh majority. One needs to add in the same breath, of course, that Moscow played ball. It never claimed the Russian-populated territories or gave support to those few within Kazakhstan who wanted to secede and join the Russian Federation. However, things are less stable along Uzbekistan's borders with Kyrgyzstan and Tajikistan. The dispute over water rights between Tashkent and Dushanbe, Tajikistan, which flared up again at the end of 2009, represents a particularly dangerous type of potential interstate conflict in Central Asia.

What this broad-brush picture demonstrates is that the region, which was once described as a cauldron of tensions and compared to the Balkans,[2] has been doing better over a 20-year stretch, than many have expected. The governments everywhere in Central Asia look strong but are vulnerable to rivalries at the top, especially at the time of a leader's death, and to challenges from below, often led by Islamist groups. Yet, 2 decades after the fall of the USSR, each former Soviet republic of the region has managed to become a full-fledged state — complete with recognized borders and a crude sense of identity within them — and a member of the international community: the United Nations (UN) and the Organization for Security and Co-operation in Europe (OSCE) memberships at independence, the Shanghai Cooperation Organization (SCO), the CIS, Collective Security Treaty Organization (CSTO), Organization of Economic Development, Caspian summits, *et al*.

Among the countries of Central Asia, Kazakhstan has taken the lead on several fronts: post-Soviet

—"Eurasian"—integration with Russia; continental Asian—focused on confidence building; and pan-European, where, in 2010, it became the first OSCE chair among the new independent states of the ex-USSR. Turkmenistan, at the other extreme, has managed to get a formal UN recognition of its "neutral" status. Kyrgyzstan has become the first and so far only member of the World Trade Organization (WTO) in Central Asia. All five are weak states, for sure, yet none today is a failing one, although Kyrgyzstan has come close.

CENTRAL ASIA COMES INTO ITS OWN

At the beginning of the 21st century, Central Asia began attracting more international attention than it has received for decades, even centuries. There are two principal reasons for this: hydrocarbons and security. Even though the exuberant reports in the 1990s that suggested that the Caspian was a second Gulf turned out to be vastly exaggerated, the oil and gas resources of Kazakhstan, Turkmenistan, and Uzbekistan are substantial. They are of interest to several major outside players, Russia, America, China, and Europe. In security terms, Central Asia, a predominantly Muslim region directly adjacent to the Greater Middle East and, in particular, Afghanistan and Iran, is a staging ground and a potential battlefield in the confrontation between Muslim radicals and moderates, Western military forces, and jihadists.

It has become fashionable to talk about a new Great Game in Central Asia. Modeled on the 19th century geopolitical context,[3] the new Game pits Russian interests against those of the United States, or, in another version, Russia, America, and China are seen as engaging in a three-corner competition. This view, apparently well-rooted in the region's history, misses a vital dimension: the Central Asia states themselves. In the previous cycle, throughout the 19th and early 20th centuries, Central Asians were but objects, playthings, prizes to be won or lost by the great power rivals, the British and Russian empires. Today, things are different.

At this stage in their evolution, Central Asians can and do decide how to orient themselves in the international environment. Of course, they have to take the existing realities into account, but so do all others. Russia is a former imperial hegemon, mentor, and model, with many links still tying it to the region. China is an economic powerhouse second to none on the Asian continent. Both Russia and China, the hegemonic power until the 18th century, are the two big immediate neighbors, and the United States, the current global power, is present in the region politically, economically, and militarily.[4] Since 2001, it has been engaged in an operation in the neighboring Afghanistan. Turkey stands for a secular Muslim state model, Iran, for the model of an Islamist state. Both countries have ethnic brethren in Central Asia who are watching them. The European Union (EU) has been paying increasing attention to the region, mostly for economic reasons, as have such Asian majors as the rich Japan and the rising India. The latter's interest is not only economic, but also geopolitical.

As a result, all Central Asian countries have naturally developed multivector foreign policies. Kazakhstan, Russia's only direct neighbor—across a border that runs for over 7,500 km and is the world's longest—and an integration partner within the Euro-Asian Economic Community and the Customs Union, has been carefully and successfully maneuvering among China,

Russia, and the United States. Symbolically and tell-ingly, it has been pumping its oil via the Baku-Ceyhan pipeline to Europe, the Caspian Pipeline Consortium (CPC) outlet to Russia, and a new pipeline to China.

Uzbekistan, the region's heartland and its most populous country, was compelled in the mid-2000s to reorient itself away from the United States and to-ward Russia and China, but it can hardly be taken for granted by Moscow or Beijing. As a transit country for Afghanistan-bound North Atlantic Treaty Organi-zation (NATO) traffic, Uzbekistan seeks to maintain relations with European nations, including Germany, France, and Spain. Tashkent moves back and forth, but its goal is to stay independent of any one of the bigger nations, and become a regional power in its own right.

Turkmenistan, after its abrupt 2006 power change, has been emerging cautiously from its 15-year isola-tion to look for the best possible deals from its potential customers in Russia, China, and the West. Tajikistan has been pursuing a foreign policy *tous azimuths*. It is formally allied with Russia, and informally aligned with Iran, which is a kind of cultural patron as a fellow Persian-speaking country. Dushanbe, however, is also reaching out to the West, the United States in particu-lar, and to India, who leases an airbase at Ayni. Kyr-gyzstan, the region's smallest nation, is also unique in the sense that it has been hosting both U.S. and Rus-sian military bases a mere 20 miles apart. When the U.S.-Russian relations soured, Bishkek managed to perform a juggling act by keeping the Americans (and the revenue from the base) in; and the Russians happy by offering them an additional base in the south of the country, if they could pay.

Thus, Central Asians, while not the big movers and shakers themselves, are sufficiently autonomous on the international scene. They are not mere pawns in someone else's game and should not be taken for granted by the bigger powers.

OUTSIDERS' POLICIES TOWARD CENTRAL ASIA IN THE 1990S

Since 1991, Russia's policies toward the region have changed several times. Moscow started with a policy of benign neglect. It began a slow-motion retreat throughout the region. The new states had to learn to live without Moscow, and manage their own affairs, domestic and foreign, themselves. President Boris Yeltsin and his liberal reformers basically saw Central Asians as a drag for reaching their initial central goal of reintegration into the West. Soon, however, Moscow had to pay more attention to Central Asia, as a result of the violent conflict in Tajikistan, where it intervened in force to ensure the victory of Rakhmon's communist faction. In the mid-to late-1990s, Tajikistan was regarded in Moscow as the front line of defense against the Afghan Taliban who captured Kabul, Afghanistan, in 1996. The small Russian force deployed in Tajikistan (an understrength motor rifle division plus Russian-led border guards) was the only capable military formation between Afghanistan and Russia's southern border a thousand miles north.

In the 1990s, the Kremlin was only intimating post-Soviet economic integration in Central Asia, without a serious intention or sufficient resources to turn this formal objective into a reality. It was only in the 2000s that Moscow has become more realistic with regard to what it hopes to achieve in the region, and the ways of achieving these goals. Moscow also discovered that it was no longer the only outside player in the region by far.

The United States, which recognized all the new states at their inception as part of a wider policy to cement the deimperialization of Russia, started paying attention to some Central Asian countries in the mid- to late-1990s as the Caspian emerged on the world energy map. NATO, under the Partnership for Peace program, established formal contacts with all countries of the region except for Turkmenistan. It helped train their small joint military force, the Central Asian Battalion (CENTRASBAT), which was to be a token of regional military cooperation and of the region's security outreach to the West.

China, for its part, emphasized security, trade development, and energy. It completed the process of border fixation and border demilitarization, which had started when the Soviet Union was still in existence, with the broken Union's successor states. Beijing's goal was not only to regulate borders with neighbors, but to demilitarize them — in particular with the Russian Federation. Where Central Asian states were concerned, it sought to make sure that these Turkic-speaking Muslim neighbors did not become sanctuaries or safe havens for the Uighur separatists that threatened Beijing's control of Xinjiang, also known as Eastern Turkestan.

Turkey tried to raise its profile among the Turkic-speaking states, all Central Asian with the exception of Tajikistan. It soon became clear though, Ankara, while offering a secular modernization model for Muslim countries, lacked the resources to emerge as the principal patron of the region. Also, during the 1990s, despite a brief surge of pan-Turkic sentiments, Turkey was very focused on acceding to the EU.

In relative terms, Iran's involvement with Central Asia was much smaller. Technologically or socially,

Tehran's powers of attraction were limited. Also, only one country, Tajikistan, is Persian-speaking. Tehran, however, brokered the Tajik peace agreement, in cooperation with Moscow. It also established neighborly relations with insular Turkmenistan: a gas pipeline and a rail link made sure that the latter's Soviet-era isolation from its direct neighbor to the south was finally broken. Yet, until 2001 Central Asia was essentially an international backwater.

CENTRAL ASIA AFTER SEPTEMBER 11, 2001

It all changed with the events of September 11, 2001 (9/11). As Afghanistan was targeted by the United States as the home of al Qaeda, which enjoyed the hospitality and support of the extremist Taliban regime, Central Asia became a front-line region in the global war on terror.

Russia cooperated with the United States and gave practical support to Operation ENDURING FREEDOM. Moscow facilitated Washington's outreach to the Afghan Northern Alliance, which became the bulk of the anti-Taliban force on the ground. It provided intelligence information. It did not try to prevent the United States from reaching agreement with its nominal allies in the CSTO on basing rights to the U.S. military in those countries' territories.

Russia took a low profile in Afghanistan. It supported the 2001 Bonn accords on the domestic political arrangements for post-Taliban Afghanistan. It recognized Hamid Karzai, a U.S. candidate, as the new top leader in Afghanistan and was content to see its own friends from the Northern Alliance sidelined. It did not seek to undermine the new Afghan authorities. It resisted the temptation to return to Afghanistan in force as part of the international intervention. It did not even reopen its embassy in Kabul, closed when the Taliban arrived in 1996, until 2007. Moscow's focus was squarely on Central Asia. Since the early 2000s, it started to think about making a comeback, as a great power this time, rather than an empire.

Within Central Asia, Russia's interests in its five component countries — Kazakhstan, Uzbekistan, Kyrgyzstan, Tajikistan, and Turkmenistan — vary widely, as do the countries themselves. These interests are discussed by country.

Kazakhstan.

Kazakhstan is, for Russia, the most important country by far. It, rather than Russia (which readily claims the title for itself), is the quintessential Eurasian state. Geographically, demographically, and economically, northern Kazakhstan is an extension of southern Siberia and the Urals. The border was only delimited in 2005. Trains running between central Russia and Siberia have to cross Kazakhstan's borders several times during their east-west journey. The border in the Caspian Sea, fixed in a 1998 separate deal, cuts through a major gas field (Astrakhan-Atyrau). Policing such a border is almost a mission impossible. Protection and, if need be, defense of the Russian territory require a close security and defense alliance with Kazakhstan. A vast and sparsely populated country, Kazakhstan is a useful buffer between Russia and the more fervently Muslim countries of what used to be called Middle Asia to the south, and China to the east.[5]

Ethnic Russians make up just under one-third of Kazakhstan's population. Many of them live in the industrial centers of northern Kazakhstan. Thus, the Russian-Kazakhstani border cuts through a territory with a majority or near-majority Russian population. Moscow's interest, however, is not to divide Kazakhstan and annex its Russophone northern portion. The Russians know that would be courting disaster, and not only did Moscow refrain from stirring trouble, but it actively assisted its neighbor in stamping out nascent Russophone irredentism. Russia's clear interest is to help Kazakhstan succeed as a viable multi-ethnic state. Moscow believes that the significant ethnic Russian element in Kazakhstan, though its members are now effectively barred from occupying high positions in the state, is a solid link binding the two countries together.

Kazakhstan is the energy-richest country in Central Asia and thus potentially a partner in Russia's drive to become an energy superpower. The Russo-Kazakhstani agreement on dividing the Caspian bolsters Moscow's position vis-à-vis the other littoral states.

The economies of the Russian and Kazakhstani border regions are closely intertwined. In the words of Kazak authors, this extreme interconnectedness has few, if any, parallels among other pairings in the post-Soviet space. Actually, Soviet Kazakhstan's first capital, in the 1920s, was located in Orenburg, in the southern Urals. Major Russian industrial centers such as Samara, Chelyabinsk, Omsk, and Novosibirsk are situated in close proximity to the Kazakhstani border. Just across the border in Kazakhstan, Uralsk, Aktyubinsk, Qostanay, Pavlodar, Semipalatinsk, and Ust-Kamenogorsk, are all Russia-built and still predominantly Russian-populated industrial centers. Indeed, Kazakhstan is the only CIS country that can be integrated with Russia, in economic terms. In 2010, Kazakhstan and Russia, alongside Belarus, laid the groundwork for a Customs Union.

Kazakhstan's founding leader, Nazarbayev, has long been an advocate of a Eurasian Union, by which he means a close but equitable relationship with Russia and other CIS countries. In principle, this dovetails with Moscow's ambition to create a cohesive power center in the CIS. However, there is much disagreement over the actual terms of engagement, and rights of the engaging parties. Nazarbayev, while an advocate of close relations with Russia, is at the same time a staunch opponent of Russia's imperialism. He would not hear of a Greater Russia incorporating its former borderlands.

In a geopolitical master stroke in 1997, Nazarbayez transferred Kazakhstan's capital from Almaty in the south of the country to Astana, formerly Akmolinsk/ Tselinograd, close to the Russian border. Thus, he brought the government closer to the main industrial centers, reinvigorated the government bureaucracy and the political elite, and, most importantly, consolidated Kazakhstan's control over its Russian-populated northern regions.

Even more, Kazakhstan is essentially engaged in a careful balancing act among its three principal partners, Russia, China, and the United States. This maneuvering is not a zero-sum game. In fact, making a clear choice in Russia's favor is hardly a realistic proposition. At the other extreme, turning Kazakhstan into a geopolitical battlefield among the great powers is utterly destabilizing. In the Central Asian context, Kazakhstan has grown self-confident, even somewhat arrogant toward its neighbors.

Uzbekistan.

Uzbekistan, the region's most populous nation, lies just outside of the Russian integration perimeter. However, it is the key element of Middle Asia — a Russian term to denote Central Asia minus Kazakhstan. In Tsarist and Soviet times, Tashkent functioned as the informal capital of the region and a gateway to the Middle East and South Asia. It was also the principal center of the region's industry and culture and, following the rebuilding after the devastating 1966 earthquake, the Soviet showcase for the Third World.

Ever since the break-up of the USSR, Uzbekistan has been most sensitive about its sovereign status. Not to be forgotten is that much of Uzbekistan, unique among Central Asian countries, continued to be semi-independent until the early 1920s. Ancient states with long histories, Bukhara and Khiva were Russian protectorates ruled by the local emirs and khans; after the Bolshevik revolution both were, briefly, people's republics. Bukhara was, traditionally, the spiritual center of the region.

Uzbekistan's main significance to Russia now is that it is the linchpin of regional stability. As a frontline state in the battle against religious extremism, it is very vulnerable. Should Uzbekistan yield to Islamist radicalism, Middle Asia would also be swamped by it, and southern Kazakhstan seriously threatened. A strong regime in Tashkent, Moscow believes, is a bulwark against militant Islamism.

The Russians would eventually have to recognize that Uzbekistan is an heir to a long tradition of Central Asian statehood. All medieval khanates had their capitals in what is now Uzbek territory: Bukhara, Samarkand, Khiva, and Kokand. Those countries' emirs and khans have had difficult relations with Russia. Uzbekistan's present leadership has adopted Tamerlane, a 15th century ruler who built an empire through conquest, as a national hero and towering historical figure. Tamerlane, or Timur, is remembered in Russia as one belonging to the succession of ruthless invaders, in the same category as Genghis Khan and his grandson Batu, who subjugated Russia.

Uzbekistan aspires to a hegemonic role in the region. Outside of Central Asia itself, it was playing an active role in Afghanistan until 1998, supporting the forces of an ethnic Uzbek, General Abdul Rashid Dostum.

Tashkent certainly does not want to return to the Moscow fold. From 1991, Tashkent was adamant that Russia's influence in Uzbekistan be reduced. In 1998, Karimov publicly denounced Russian security services, accusing them of meddling in Uzbekistan's internal affairs. No Russian military presence in Uzbekistan was allowed, even after the 1999 terrorist attacks in Tashkent and 2000 Islamist raids when Karimov warmed up to Moscow and hosted Vladimir Putin's visits. After 9/11, Karimov firmly aligned Uzbekistan with the United States, signing an agreement in 2002 on the use of bases, such as Karshi-Khanabad (K-2).

Karimov's 2005 move to align Uzbekistan with Russia was a decision taken in extremis. After the bloody riots in Andijon, he became convinced of U.S. involvement in attempts to dislodge him. Subsequent U.S. criticism of the use of force by the Uzbek government was tantamount to pushing Tashkent into Moscow' arms. However, had Putin rejected the Karimov plea, the Uzbek leader would have probably aligned his country with China — that would have been his only option. Uzbekistan's accession to the SCO in

2000 allowed Tashkent to better handle both Beijing and Moscow. It was to Beijing that Karimov flew in May 2005, a few days after the Andijon rebellion. The decision in favor of Russia is now being revisited by Karimov himself.

Russia's interest cannot be Uzbekistan's integration. However, a solid relationship with Tashkent is important for Moscow if it wants to somehow manage the situation in the region. Populous, less rich in natural resources, and endowed with a surviving industrial base, Uzbekistan is also a market for Russian goods and services and a partner for joint ventures.

Kyrgyzstan.

The two small states, Kyrgyzstan and Tajikistan, are important to Russia as its forward positions in the region, blocking hostile entry into Central Asia from the outside. Kyrgyzstan is a country where Russian, Chinese, and American interests intersect. The United States and Russia maintain military bases there, virtually side by side; China has probably been interested in getting one for itself. Economically, northern Kyrgyzstan is an extension of Kazakhstan, also with a sizeable Russian population. By contrast, southern Kyrgyzstan, with the small portion of Ferghana valley that it controls, is closely linked with Uzbekistan, Afghanistan, and Tajikistan. Moscow has been trying hard to reduce U.S. official and nongovernmental organization (NGO)-sponsored influence in Kyrgyzstan, which is highest in the region. However, during the 2010 political turmoil in Kyrgyzstan—the toppling of President Bakiyev and the disturbances in the southern city of Osh, complete with anti-Uzbek pogroms— Russian and U.S. policies were brought into a kind of harmony. The reset in U.S.-Russian relations has had an effect on Central Asia, too.

Tajikistan.

Tajikistan used to be seen as Russia's checkpoint on the Afghan border. During the 1990s, it was also the main supply base for the anti-Taliban Northern Alliance. With the arrival of U.S. and NATO forces in Afghanistan and the transformation of the principal security threat to Central Asia, which now takes the form of domestic rebellions rather than cross-border attacks, the importance of Tajikistan has changed. Initially, it was briefly a principal gateway to Afghanistan. Later, however, it came to be primarily seen as the first station in the long route of Afghan drugs traffic, which has been expanding dramatically since the fall of the Taliban. On the positive side, Tajikistan, alongside with Kyrgyzstan, is key to the control of the region's water resources. In the future, the importance of the water factor is likely to rise, and Russia is certainly interested in winning a commanding position for itself.

Tajikistan is the only Persian-speaking nation in Central Asia. Its long and bloody civil war was put to rest in 1997 through joint efforts of Moscow and Tehran. Tajiks are a significant ethnic group in Afghanistan, whose leader, Ahmad Shah Massoud, fought against the Soviet army during the Afghan war, and later became the rallying figure in the anti-Taliban resistance and an American ally. In the post-9/11 situation, Tajikistan has offered to host NATO air forces engaged in Afghanistan. Its long-time President, Emommali Rakhmon, a nominal Russian ally, carefully maneuvers among all the players in the region, including the United States, Iran, China, Pakistan, Afghanistan, and India, not to forget its powerful neighbor, Uzbekistan.

Turkmenistan.

Finally, Turkmenistan is, above all, a major natural gas producer that Russia wants to keep tied to its gas pipeline system. This link is also an important factor contributing to Moscow's virtual monopoly on gas supply to Ukraine. With Turkmenistan's southern border mostly with Iran, Russia does not insist on a military presence there. In fact, Russia let the city of Ashgabat quietly ease its way out from the country, which once hosted a major Soviet garrison. However, Moscow did not mind Turkmenistan's neutrality as long as it did not offer military base facilities to the United States. Even Niyazov's decision in August 2005 to downgrade Turkmenistan's status in the CIS from a full member to an observer did not cause much of a stir on the Russian side. Evidently, Turkmenbashi's maverick dictatorship is a less serious problem for Moscow than either an overtly Islamist or a pro-Western regime.

Overall, today's Russia is pursuing a policy of economic expansionism in Central Asia, with a strong energy accent to it. It seeks to tie Kazakh, Turkmen, and Uzbek oil and gas resources to its market and its pipeline network. It has concluded agreements with Astana, Ashgabat, and Tashkent on a Caspian coastal pipeline. It weathered a long spat with Ashgabat over gas supplies/prices in 2008, but has finally concluded a deal with it. Russian companies, many owned by the state, have been investing in the region, seeking control over its energy production. Moscow founded a Euro-Asian Economic Community, to which Kazakhstan, Kyrgyzstan, and Tajikistan belong (Uzbekistan remains a maverick), and a Customs Union with Kazakhstan and, beyond Central Asia, Belarus. Russia has revamped the 1992 Tashkent treaty and founded a smaller, but tighter CSTO. It established a small air presence at Kant, Kyrgyzstan.

The Russian leaders clearly prefer the status quo in Central Asian states to any attempts to overthrow it. This preference does not result from any ideological affinity or some sentimental authoritarian solidarity. In the prevailing Russian government view, the ruling authoritarians are unlikely to be succeeded by enlightened democrats; rather, they may be overthrown by Islamist radicals. It is religious extremism that is defined as the clear and present danger facing the region.

Moscow looks with a wary eye at U.S. activities in the region. It suspected U.S.-affiliated NGOs of having had a hand in the February 2005 toppling of President Askar Akayev of Kyrgyzstan. Even though the Russians managed the situation well for themselves, and moved swiftly to establish close relations with the new regime in Bishkek, they remained suspicious of U.S. policies in the region. The Kremlin exploited the May 2005 Andijon rebellion to help the Uzbek President Karimov distance himself from the United States and the West. The Kremlin then hoped Uzbekistan would return to the Russian sphere of influence. From 2005, Russia started to call into question the U.S. military presence in Central Asia and made statements suggesting it was time for Americans to go.

To many in Russia, by the mid-2000s at the latest, Central Asia—wrongly, in this author's view—had become a battleground in the new Great Game, this time waged by Moscow and Washington. Russia, however, took a kindlier attitude to China's insertion into the region. This can be explained by a shift in Russia's overall strategy. During most of the 2000s, the center of gravity of Russian policy had been moving from west to east. The United States, while remaining central, has also become more distant. The EU, having expanded to include much of Europe outside the CIS, is politically confused and economically stagnant. Asia, by contrast, is demonstrating dynamism. The West is not alone in its preoccupation with the rise of China and India. The Russians, too, are looking for opportunities even as they are preparing to face the concomitant challenges.

In Russia's eyes, China has greatly grown in stature in the last 15 years, more starkly even than the West. Historically regarded as huge but essentially inferior to Russia, China has, within a decade and a half, achieved formal equality with, and informal superiority over, its former hegemon and mentor. In the mid-2000s, China joined the United States and the EU as one of Russia's three principal global partners.

By moving closer to China, Russia hopes to escape America's tutelage. Its strategy could be described as leaning on the East to raise one's stakes in the West. At the same time, Russia wants to avoid becoming China's satellite. The calculus is that, for the foreseeable future, Beijing, focused on China's domestic development, will be taking a relatively low profile internationally. This will buy time for Moscow. By the time China becomes more assertive, Russia will have strengthened itself and consolidated its zone of vital interests.

Central Asia is a major area of Russo-Chinese interaction. It was with regard to that region that the SCO was founded. Originally, the SCO could well be dubbed China in Central Asia, but Russia found the SCO formula much to its liking. Under the arrangement, Moscow and Beijing share leadership in a group that also includes all countries of Central Asia except Turkmenistan, and acts as a platform which attracts the major powers of continental Asia. In the Kremlin's mind, the SCO is a useful counterweight to growing U.S./Western presence in Eurasia. Over time, its purpose has expanded alongside with its geographical scope. Along with China, Russia and four Central Asian countries are SCO members, including India, Pakistan, Iran, and Mongolia as observers. At least *in potentia*, some Russians believe, the SCO could become an alternative to the U.S.-led international community (North America, Western and Central Europe, Japan, and Australia). Thus, for the first time since the fall of the Berlin wall, a new global geopolitical set-up may be emerging.

Whatever China's strategy, Beijing's tactics were strikingly circumspect, respectful of Moscow's sensitivities, and highlighting cooperation. China's 2000 initiative of institutionalizing the border normalization talks, which had led to a 1996 agreement, as a regional council, the SCO.

RUSSIA'S VIEWS OF U.S. FOREIGN POLICY UNDER THE OBAMA ADMINISTRATION

The resetting of U.S.-Russian relations in early 2009 was a result of a more general overhaul of the U.S. foreign policy during the transition from the President George W. Bush administration to President Barack Obama and his people. Moscow, for its part, did not believe it had to change its overall approach to relations with the United States. "You break it, you fix it" was the general attitude in the Russian government toward the need to improve U.S.-Russian relations at the end of the Bush administration. The famous "reset button" that Secretary of State Hillary Clinton presented to Foreign Minister Sergei Lavrov when they met in Geneva in March 2009 had an incorrect translation into Russian, as good a proof as any that the Russians had had no finger in *that* pie before they were invited to press it.

On the whole, the Russian leadership saw President Barack Obama's foreign policy as a much-needed correction of the overextension of American power under President Bush. Russia's central interests dealt with U.S. policies toward NATO enlargement to Ukraine and Georgia, U.S. support for Tbilisi, and ballistic missile defense plans in Europe and on the global scale. On all those issues, Washington moved in 2009 basically to accommodate Moscow's concerns. However, all decisions by the Obama administration, being unilateral and requiring no concessions from the Russians, are also fully sovereign. They are essentially stay-decisions which can be revisited when and if Washington decides it needs to move forward.

By mid-2010, Russia's foreign policy had gone through its own parallel reset. Rather than an instrument to shore up Russia's diminishing status in global affairs, it was decreed to be a vehicle for drawing resources from the outside world for aiding Moscow's technological modernization drive. This reprioritized Russian foreign policy, which became focused, once again, on relations with the leading EU member states—Germany, France, and Italy—as well as the United States, in what President Medevedev called "modernization alliances."[6]

Within that general setting, Moscow interprets the new U.S. strategies for Iraq and Afghanistan as a reconfiguration of American presence, a dramatic drawdown of Western military engagement in the former and one last push in the latter, but not a complete withdrawal from the region. The Russian leaders realize full well that the Obama administration needs Moscow's cooperation on Afghanistan and Iran, and dispenses carefully its small steps toward the United States. Moscow, however, does not feel compelled to follow the U.S. lead without reservation. It is resolved to remain an independent strategic actor.

As far as Iran is concerned, Russia is somewhat less worried than the United States about Tehran's nuclear program. It also views U.S. heightened concerns as a reflection of Israel's, which are existential in nature. In the part of the world living under the constant threat of an Indo-Pakistani nuclear exchange, and Pakistan's potential nuclear meltdown as a result of domestic implosion, Iran's nuclear threat does not loom that large. The prospect of nuclear proliferation in the region is interpreted as a weak argument: in case of Iran's nuclearization, extended U.S. deterrence offering protection to the Gulf States is seen as a more likely outcome. The United States, the Russians feel, has enough leverage in Egypt to dissuade it from going nuclear; as for Turkey, Ankara's decisions are taken with a view to its wider interests in continued alliance with Washington and complicated relations with the EU.

This does not mean that Russia supports Iran's nuclear ambitions, or connives with Tehran. There is no love lost between the two. Moscow senses Tehran's contempt for its reduced power status, and hardens its stance occasionally if only not to be dismissed or taken for granted by the Iranians. Russia, however, sees Iran as a rising regional power that would be a formidable adversary if Moscow alienates it. It also sees Iran as a more or less rational actor, which occasionally can be a partner. Several Russian companies have some interests in Iran, which may be modest in absolute terms, but irreplaceable if Russia succumbs to Washington's calls and agrees to impose harsh sanctions against Tehran. In more general terms, few people in Moscow want to make life easier for the United States, and, unlike a decade ago, there are no serious voices pleading for a strategic alignment with Washington. Tactical cooperation, in a strictly *quid pro quo* manner, is still deemed possible, and occasionally desirable, but a U.S.-Russian strategic marriage is out of the question. This applies not only to Iran, but also to Afghanistan.

RUSSIA'S PERCEIVED INTERESTS IN AFGHANISTAN

Russia views Afghanistan today largely through the prism of security threats to itself and its Central Asian neighborhood where Moscow aspires to soft dominance.[7] Afghanistan is also an element of Russia's complex and complicated relations with the United States and NATO. Finally, the Afghanistan-Pakistan situation impacts on Russia's relations with major non-Western powers, such as China, India, Iran, and Saudi Arabia. In the Russian political mind, rational calculations of interests and analyses of threats are superimposed, of course, on the Soviet Union's traumatic experience in Afghanistan (the "Afghan syndrome"), and on the post-Soviet Russian experience in Chechnya, Dagestan, Ingushetia, and Tajikistan.

In terms of perceived threats, two stand out. One is the prospect of instability in Central Asia, which would follow should the Karzai government fall and the U.S./NATO military forces withdraw precipitously. This scenario carries a sense of *déjà vu*: the Taliban had once come to power in Afghanistan, which encouraged Central Asian Islamists and offered training camps to Chechen rebels. Russia fears a rise in Islamic radicalism across the region and a revival of rebel activity in Uzbekistan and Kyrgyzstan. It does not have sufficient confidence either in the solidity of Central Asian regimes or in its own capacity to insulate the region from the influence of a victorious Taliban. Still, opinions differ in Russia as to how far the threat can reach. While some Russians espouse a kind of a domino theory and expect the disaster area to spread all the way to Russia's own borders, most believe the Taliban will not expand far beyond Afghanistan itself.

The other threat is even more real, and deadly — drugs trafficking from Afghanistan. Recently, Russia has stopped being a drugs transit country par excellence and has become a major consumer of Afghan heroin and opiates. According to the UN, Russian annual consumption of heroin (70 tons) is only slightly less than the consumption of the rest of Europe combined (88 tons).[8] Out of about 100,000 drug addicts dying each year worldwide, 30-40,000 people are Russians. Russian officials point out that the production of narcotics in Afghanistan has grown exponentially (44 times, according to the Russian government's anti-drug Czar, Viktor Ivanov), since the fall of the Taliban and the arrival of the coalition forces.[9] They are genuinely worried.

By way of contrast, Moscow has relatively little interest in Afghanistan, per se. Historically, Russians had been content for decades with Afghanistan being a buffer zone between their empire in Central Asia and Britain's in India. They appreciated Afghanistan's neutrality in the Cold War, when both Pakistan and Iran were U.S. allies, and China was locked in its own Cold War-style conflict with the Soviet Union. They were surprised by the leftist coup that proclaimed Afghanistan a Moscow client, and intervened only reluctantly when that regime threatened to disintegrate and create an opening for the United States. The painful decade-long Soviet intervention over, the Russians preferred to forget about Afghanistan — until the Taliban arrived. At present, Russia's aims in Afghanistan include prevention, essentially by the U.S.-led coalition, of an outright victory for the Taliban; stemming the flow of drugs out of Afghanistan, especially into Russia; and restoring a pacified and neutral Afghanistan as a buffer state between Central Asia and the Greater Middle East.

Russia's current economic interests in Afghanistan are modest. The trade turnover is just under $200 million (2008). In principle, Russia would be interested in exploiting oil and gas fields discovered by Soviet geologists in the country's north. However, at present Russian business groups would prefer, if anything, to invest in neighboring Central Asia, which is richer in all kinds of resources, much more familiar to the Russians and immensely safer than Afghanistan. Russians also tend to believe, wrongly perhaps, that U.S. influence in Afghanistan minimizes their chances of doing business there. Moreover, China has emerged as a formidable economic rival to Russia in Afghanistan. It defeated Russian companies in the tender for the Ainak copper reserve, one of the biggest in the world. Ironically, Russia's *negative* interests in Afghanistan are more important than positive ones, e.g., in order to protect its markets, Gazprom seeks to block projects of a gas pipeline from Turkmenistan to Pakistan, and even of an oil pipeline from Pakistan's port city of Gwadar to China.[10]

Russia's interests in Afghanistan are mostly concentrated in the north of the country, with its largely Tajik and Uzbek populations. There, Russia continues to cultivate the close ties it had developed with the Northern Alliance. Afghanistan's north is directly linked to Central Asia, which Russia seeks to keep within its orbit. This is Moscow's paramount interest in the region. This ambition, however, outstrips Russia's available means. Russia does not work as a magnet for its neighbors. For their part, Central Asian countries do not want to be seen as Moscow's clients, their refusal to recognize Abkhazia and South Ossetia richly attests to that. Russia, however, has been playing on the Central Asians' concerns over Afghanistan again becoming a base for their domestic radicalism. This is being done to increase Russia's own military and security presence in the region, and to beef up the Moscow-led CSTO. If not the Taliban itself, then the threat of a Taliban victory in Afghanistan supports Russian interests in Central Asia.

RUSSIA'S POLICIES IN AFGHANISTAN IN SUPPORT OF ITS INTERESTS

Publicly, Russia supports the international effort to stabilize the situation in Afghanistan. In December 2009, President Medvedev publicly endorsed Obama's new strategy for Afghanistan and offered Russia's support for Kabul, Washington, and NATO.[11]

Moscow is gratified that the international operation has a UN mandate and that the parameters of

Afghanistan's post-Taliban rehabilitation were laid down at the Bonn conference in which Moscow participated. Even though a number of senior Russians would privately like to see the United States fail in Afghanistan and join the Soviet Union and Britain in the graveyard of empires, pragmatic Russian leaders realize that a Western defeat in Afghanistan would result in a rise of radicalism, which they themselves would not be able to contain. However, the idea of sending Russian forces to Afghanistan is roundly rejected by the Russian government, the bulk of the country's political establishment, and the general public. The Afghan Syndrome is still strong, 20 years after the Soviet withdrawal from the country.

Beyond that, opinions differ within the Russian establishment. Those who see the United States as Russia's main geopolitical adversary, want the United States to stay bogged down in Afghanistan indefinitely, preventing a Taliban victory yet still unable to prevail themselves. They favor a policy of watching the Afghan developments from the sidelines, giving no serious assistance to the U.S./NATO forces there, and ready to cut a deal with the Taliban should it emerge in a strong position in the end. On the other end of the spectrum are those who advocate much closer cooperation with the United States and NATO on Afghanistan. They hope that, by becoming a friend to the United States during its time of need, they would be able to sway Washington's policy on the issues of principal importance to Moscow, mostly in the former Soviet Union; to the first group, this view looks naïve. A third group, composed of more straightforward thinkers, believes that Russia is interested in the coalition victory in Afghanistan for its own sake, since that would remove the most serious external challenge to date to Russia's own security. The result of the inter-play of these basic positions has been Moscow giving support, but modest, to the Afghan government and the coalition.

Russia has maintained regular contacts with Kar-zai, his government officials, and some local warlords to keep itself abreast of the developments in the coun-try. Moscow has extended some military assistance to Kabul. It has expressed willingness to train Afghan police and military officers, and sell the Afghan gov-ernment arms, military equipment, and spare parts. In the future, Russia plans to make a comeback in Af-ghanistan (it established its embassy there in 2007), but hedges its bets, unsure about Karzai's longevity or the Western commitment. It does not want to run afoul of new Afghan authorities, should the present ones be replaced. By pursuing such a course, it hopes to win a measure of political influence, mostly to en-sure that Afghanistan is not used by others against Russian interests, including in the economic area. Un-til recently, Russia has enjoyed sympathies of a group of senior Afghans it befriended in the 1980s and the 1990s. Moscow, however, neglected to use the oppor-tunity of turning this group into something like a pro-Russian lobby.

Russia has signed agreements with the United States, Germany, France, and Spain allowing transit of nonlethal military goods and, in some cases, person-nel, weapons, and military equipment, across Russian territory; by rail, and through the air space with up to 4,500 flights per annum.[12] Thus, Russia sought both to increase its value in the eyes of the United States and to demonstrate the privileged nature of its relations with some of the key countries of continental Europe.

Russia has been trying to engage the United States on the drugs-trafficking issue. It believes that curtailing production of opium inside Afghanistan is the most effective way of handling the issue. Beyond Afghanistan's borders, Russian officials claim the price of drugs becomes simply prohibitive for fighting their trafficking. High degrees of corruption in Russia and Central Asian countries and low efficiency of the anti-drug agencies are a more likely factor. According to the UN, Russia and the Central Asian states interdict only 4 and 5 percent of the traffic, respectively, far less than Iran (20 percent), Pakistan (18 percent), or China (17 percent).[13]

Moscow has long been pleading with the NATO alliance to establish alliance-to-alliance relations with the CSTO it leads. This is deemed important as a sign of Western recognition of Russia's politico-military primacy in Central Asia. The support to this idea given by Zbigniew Brzezinski notwithstanding, NATO has shown little interest in it. Acting on its own, Russia has transformed its understrength motor rifle division into a small military base in Tajikistan on the Afghan border and has established a small air base at Kant, Kyrgyzstan. It has also been looking for another base in the south of that country, which it wants to turn into a CSTO outpost.

At the same time, Russia has been trying to diminish the U.S. military footprint in Central Asia. In 2005, it used the SCO to demand an end to the U.S. military presence in Central Asia. It leaned on Kyrgyzstan to follow the Uzbek example and expel the U.S. forces. However, the more recent intensification of fighting in Afghanistan and the need to enhance U.S./NATO forces there, which Russia basically supports, is at odds with its desire to see the back of the U.S. military in Central Asia. The Russians have to be content with sending periodic messages — through biannual SCO military exercises conducted since 2005 — that the U.S. military are not the only game in Central Asia.

RUSSIA'S INTERESTS IN AFGHANISTAN VIS-À-VIS THOSE OF OTHER POWERS

Moscow clearly feels its position in Central Asia is challenged by others, above all by the United States, which it regards — here as well as in most other places — as *the Other*. This highlights the central contradiction of the Russian position. While the U.S./NATO operation in Afghanistan deals with a very serious security challenge to Russia, it has also made the United States a power in Central Asia — at Russia's expense, as seen from Moscow. In 2001, Putin acquiesced in the U.S. acquisition of air bases in Uzbekistan and Kyrgyzstan, but made it clear that Russia considered those deployments as temporary, only for the duration of the stabilization effort in Afghanistan.[14] However, that effort has been going on for over 8 years now.

The rise of China has challenged Russia's position in Central Asia even more massively, fundamentally, and permanently than America's insertion into the region. However, Moscow, while traditionally allergic to military expansionism, is relatively tolerant toward projection of economic influence, which distinguishes the Chinese practice in Central Asia from America's. Also, it is still the United States whom Russia regards as its principal competitor, not China. To oppose and constrain the U.S. role in the region, Moscow has been partnering with Beijing in building the SCO into a major international forum that included — beyond China, Russia, and Central Asia — key players such as India,

Pakistan, and Iran. Afghanistan, like the other three latter countries, is an observer. In March 2009, the SCO held a conference in Moscow on Afghanistan — essentially to raise its own profile. The SCO, whose budget is a mere $ 4 million, has no chance of playing a significant role within Afghanistan, including that of a mediator between the Kabul government and elements of the Taliban. Its useful specialization remains regional summitry.

Afghanistan is an issue in Russia's relations with India and Pakistan. Delhi has been Moscow's close partner, even a quasi-ally, for decades. India was one of the very few countries that refused to condemn the 1979 Soviet invasion of Afghanistan. Today, Russia has no problem with India's political presence in Afghanistan. Both countries suffer from terrorist attacks and are fighting Islamist radicals. Yet, the Indo-Russian relationship has been hollowing out. There is little consultation and virtually no coordination between the two countries on issues relating to Afghanistan. Even though Russia occasionally mounts public relations campaigns highlighting Brazil, Russia, India, and China (BRIC) and Russia, India, and China (RIC) as pillars of a post-Western world, Moscow is keenly aware of the rivalry between its two principal partners, Beijing and Delhi, and is careful not to be drawn into their disputes.

This rivalry is nowhere more intense than in relation to Pakistan. For Moscow, Pakistan had long been its principal adversary's accomplice. It served as a base for U.S. intelligence operations against the Soviet Union and, most crucially, was the main base for the Afghan resistance to the Soviet forces in Afghanistan, and the conduit for international aid to them. Russia, however, cannot afford to ignore a nuclear-armed country with a population that has recently topped Russia's own. Careful not to spoil its relationship with India, Russia has been maintaining and even expanding contacts both with the Pakistani government and its military. Yet, the Russians realize they have little knowledge and even less influence as far as Pakistan's internal dynamics are concerned. They see Pakistan as America's and China's ward, essentially, and hope that, in extremis, those two powers would prevent the worst outcome (a nuclear meltdown) from occurring.

Moscow's contacts with Tehran are broader and somewhat deeper than those with Islamabad, but also contentious. For Russia, Iran is a key regional player whose power continues to be on the rise, and an economic partner of some importance, especially in the energy sector. For all the difficulties of dealing with Iran, Russians see Iranians as essentially rational and, at times, cooperative. Moscow and Tehran cooperated to put an end to the civil war in Tajikistan—the only post-Soviet conflict that has actually been resolved. Russia certainly benefited from a benevolent Iranian attitude to Moscow's actions in Chechnya and its Russia-friendly position within the Organization of the Islamic Conference. With regard to Afghanistan, Russia sees Iran as a stabilizing factor in Herat and as a partner in curbing drugs trafficking.

Finally, Russia, in contrast to the period of its own intervention in Afghanistan, maintains a relationship with Saudi Arabia, which, while not particularly close, is active and generally friendly. Moscow has taken great pains to position itself as a friend of the Islamic world and win an observer status with the Organization of the Islamic Conference.

CAN THESE INTERESTS BE RECONCILED?

As is clear from the above, there is no antagonism between Russia's interests with reference to Afghanistan and those of any other major player. On many key issues, these interests are fairly close. Russia was a *de facto* ally of the Alliance in 2001, contributing substantially, in political and intelligence terms, to the toppling of the Taliban by the U.S.-supported Northern Alliance forces. After that, Russia chose not to meddle in Afghan politics and did not contest the U.S. influence over the Karzai administration. Russia's geopolitical rivalry with the United States is in the former Soviet republics of Central Asia, and also the Caspian and the Caucasus. Even there, however, the issue is not some new edition of the Great Game, but rather the emergence of new states in the region who aspire to genuine independence from their former hegemon and who are learning to move around on the international scene, choosing orientations and looking for balances. Russia's dream of soft dominance in Central Asia will remain a dream.

In terms of whether Moscow will support the U.S. goals in Afghanistan, it is the wider context of U.S.-Russian and, by extension, NATO-Russian relations that matters most. A NATO expanding into the former Soviet Union (Ukraine and Georgia); U.S. support for a Georgian president bent on solving ethnic conflicts in his country by force; and a U.S. plan to deploy missile defenses close to Russia's borders and with some capability of weakening the Russian deterrence capacity were not the right incentives, under the George W. Bush administration, for Russia supporting the U.S./NATO efforts in Afghanistan. There is a widely held view in Moscow — now that these irritants are off the table for the duration of the Obama administration — that the general environment of U.S.-Russian relations is now more propitious for closer collaboration on issues such as Afghanistan.

THE IMPACT OF RUSSIA'S PURSUIT OF ITS INTERESTS FOR (1) ACHIEVING STABILITY IN AFGHANISTAN, AND (2) THE SUCCESS OF COALITION GOALS AND OPERATIONS IN AFGHANISTAN

So far, Russia's policies have been generally consonant with the coalition's goal and efforts in Afghanistan. Moscow's realistic policy spectrum lies between passive and active support for the U.S. and NATO policies there. However, even Russia's more active support for the coalition operation in Afghanistan will only have a marginal impact on the outcome of the U.S.-led international involvement in that country.

Russians have different views on the present U.S. strategy in Afghanistan. Even those sympathetic to it, however, point out that the Obama strategy focuses on two issues: strengthening the Afghan government forces, and thwarting the Taliban's drive to oust it. What is missing in Washington's approach, they feel, is a dedicated effort to help an interlocutor arise on the side of the Taliban who would be willing and capable of reaching out for a settlement with Kabul and, indirectly, the United States, which would eventually stabilize the country.

AN OUTLOOK FOR THE SHORT-AND MEDIUM-TERM FUTURE

In the Greater Middle East, 2010-12 will be crucial years for U.S. policy. The future developments in Afghanistan and Iraq, Pakistan and Iran—and Middle-East-related terrorism against the United States—will probably define the fate of Obama's foreign policy.

Basically, the Russian leadership would want to see the United States out of Iraq. They would not support Washington's military action or coercive diplomacy toward Iran. They hope Israel does not try to "do another Osirak" by seeking to eliminate Iranian nuclear-related targets. On Pakistan, Russians believe the Americans and the Chinese are the only ones who could make sure that Pakistan does not unravel and turn into a nuclear mess, which would affect them. In Afghanistan, Russians are torn between their interest in having the U.S.-led coalition check the Taliban, and their general disinterest in having the United States triumph there.

In Central Asia, Russians see Americans as their principal competitors for regional primacy. In contrast to that, Moscow sees Beijing's interests in Central Asia as more legitimate—China is a neighbor—and more compatible with its own: China refrains from telling the Russians what they should be doing.

The real security problems of Central Asia are more likely to emerge within the five countries concerned rather than among the outsiders competing for influence. The potential for trouble can materialize into real trouble as a result of developments just outside Central Asia. Should the U.S.-led coalition fail to stabilize Afghanistan and leave precipitously, radicalism in Central Asia will be boosted. A disintegrated

Afghanistan would have a clear negative impact on Central Asia. Should the crisis over Iran's nuclear program lead to a U.S. or U.S.-supported military strike against Iran, Central Asia will be affected by a wave of destabilization sweeping across the region. A clash between India and Pakistan, with its nuclear overtones, will create a wholly different, and exceedingly bleak security environment in the region.

Within Central Asia, one obvious potential center of unrest is Fergana Valley, with its density of population, destitution, social deprivation, and Islamist activism in protest against the distant, unfair, and un-Islamic state. With most of the valley being part of Uzbekistan, and smaller portions owned by Tajikistan and Kyrgyzstan, the trouble can spread to several countries more or less simultaneously. Kyrgyzstan's ancient town of Osh in Fergana remains a focal point of separatism in that country, arguably the weakest state in the region. There are strong regional differences and tensions within Tajikistan, with its northern city, Khujand, also part of Fergana. Other parts of Tajikistan, such as Tavildara or Gorny Badakhshan, are only nominally controlled from Dushanbe.

Should a contingency situation along these lines emerge, the governments in place will find it difficult to deal with it. Uzbek forces were helpless in 1999-2000, when rebels marched to within 100 km of the capital, Tashkent. In 2005, they had to resort to massive use of firepower to suppress an uprising in Andijon, leading to numerous casualties. In Kyrgyzstan, in 1999 and 2000, the military and security forces were unable to deal with these same rebels. During the 2005 Tulip Revolution in Kyrgyzstan, all law-enforcement agencies, security services, and military units briefly abandoned the country to mob rule. In 2010, this scenario was repeated in Bishkek and amplified by the riots in Osh. The CSTO may have a very limited air capability against a more conventional enemy, such as organized rebel groups, but is useless against a popular uprising. The 2005 and 2010 revolutions in Bishkek and the riots in Osh were not deemed to be a CSTO case by the alliance's secretary-general himself. The idea of using Russian special police forces in an emergency, discussed in the aftermath of Andijon, is not sufficiently backed up by a requisite Russian capability, and is anyway anathema to the Uzbek leadership.

The SCO has been holding regular exercises known as Peace Missions to train Chinese, Russian, and Central Asian military in fighting a rebellion, retaking a town captured by rebels, and so on. Yet, it is not clear how well coordination will function in a real emergency. The Russians certainly have no wish to see the Chinese military operating in Central Asia; the Central Asians are cautious as to the wisdom of inviting the Russians to do the job. The most the Central Asian leaders can hope for in such cases is to be rescued, *in extremis*, by a foreign (Russian; American; or, in the future, Chinese) commando party.

CONCLUSION

Despite some tactical collaboration in Afghanistan, there is virtually no potential for serious cooperation between Russia and the United States on Central Asia. On the other hand, a new edition of the Great Game in Central Asia or, by extension, in Afghanistan is a false analogy. The future of Central Asia will not be decided by a tug-of-war between Moscow and Washington, or a tri-partite tournament with Beijing's participation.

The deciders sit also in Astana and Tashkent, as well as the other capitals of the region.

Not one of those capitals imagines itself as a Moscow satellite. This is the most adequate interpretation of their refusal to date to back the 2008 Russian recognition of Abkhazia's and South Ossetia's independence from Georgia. Not a single oil/gas producer in the region wants to depend on Russia as its sole market or a sole transit route.

By the same token, however, no Central Asian leader would think of fully and exclusively entrusting their security to the United States. Americans come, but they also move on. The color revolutions, which saw U.S.-friendly regimes in Georgia, Ukraine, and Kyrgyzstan toppled by revolutionaries proposing even friendlier policies toward the United States, were a vivid demonstration of the precariousness of the U.S. connection.

China is welcome in the region as a trading partner, investor, and lender, but feared as a potentially powerful regional hegemon. Beijing's caution and gradualism, however, blunt the feeling of a threat coming from a rising China.

As a result, Central Asians have developed a foreign policy pattern that elevates balancing and maneuvering among the major power centers — and others, such as the EU, Turkey, Iran, Pakistan, India, and Japan — to the level of a strategy.

The two leading countries of the region, Uzbekistan and Kazakhstan, also vie for regional leadership. The three other countries cannot afford to ignore those ambitions, but have no interest in subordinating themselves to the bigger neighbors. Maneuvering and balancing is thus translated onto the regional level.

In this environment, it is in Russia's interest to pursue a differentiated policy in support of its specific needs. A nostalgic territorial approach aimed at keeping the entire region in Moscow's sphere of influence is bound to fail. It also needs to develop its soft power potential to work as a power of attraction for Central Asians. Russia's enlightened self-interest calls for stability and prosperity in the region which directly and *en masse* adjoins its territory.

China will probably continue its cautious but determined policy course in support of its clear interests. Beijing will ensure that the Uigurs who became restive again in 2009 do not receive succor or sympathy across the border in Central Asia. It will expand its energy links that already provide it with oil from Kazakhstan and natural gas from Turkmenistan. In strategic terms, China is interested in building an overland energy bridge from Iran across Central Asia into western China. Such a bridge would be out of reach for both the U.S. and Indian navies, if Beijing's relations with those powers should turn sour. Chinese companies will continue to invest and expand their share of the consumer markets of Central Asian countries whose population is growing.

As both Russia and China seek to strengthen their respective positions in Central Asia in the short and medium term, Moscow and Beijing can be expected to manage their differences of interest and find ways to cooperate. In the longer term, Russia's influence will continue to decline and China's will rise — at Russia's expense, but, due to the gradual and gentle nature of the process, probably without provoking Moscow's active resistance. Central Asians themselves, unwilling to substitute a new powerful hegemon for a tired former one, will be interested in keeping some kind of balance between Chinese and Russian interests in their countries.

For the United States, Central Asia will remain, in the next few years, important in two respects: as an access way to Afghanistan, and for energy security. The fate of the U.S. mission in Afghanistan will be essentially decided during Obama's first term, although the mission will likely continue beyond that. With Afghanistan's importance to the United States receding, so will be American interests in Central Asia.

In the longer term, Washington would hardly welcome Central Asia falling back into the Russian lap, which is less probable, or its gravitation toward China, which would provide Beijing with guaranteed access to energy resources and a strategic glacis/staging ground for further geopolitical expansion. Beijing, however, will enjoy a number of advantages over the United States, and it will be careful not to offer the United States a clear reason for checking its slow but sure advance.

ENDNOTES - CHAPTER 2

1. For a good general overview of the region from a Moscow perspective, see Irina Zvyagelskaya, *Stanovlenie gosudarstv Tsentralnoy Azii: Politicheskie Processy* (*The Building of Central Asian Countries: Political Processes*), Moscow, Russia: Aspect Press, 2009.

2. In particular, see Zbigniew Brzezinski in his *Great Chessboard: American Primacy And Its Geostrategic Imperatives*, New York: Basic Books, 1998.

3. Best described in Peter Hopkirk's classic, *The Great Game: On Secret Service in High Asia*. London, UK: John Murray Publishers Ltd, 1990.

4. For an analysis of respective U.S., Russian and Chinese interests in the region, see Eugene Rumer, Dmitri Trenin, and

Huasheng Zhao, *Central Asia: Views from Washington, Moscow and Beijing*, Armonk, NY: M. E. Sharpe Inc, 2007.

5. For contrasting views of Kazakhstan, see Martha Brill Olcott, *Kazakhstan: Unfulfilled Promise*, Washington, DC: Carnegie, 2002; Roy Medvedev, *Kazakhstanskiy proryv* (*Kazakhstan's Break*), Moscow, Russia: Institute of Economic Strategies, 2007; K. K. Tokayev, *Pod styagom nezavisimosti. Ocherki o vneshney politike Kazakhstana* (*Under the Banner of Independence. Essays on Kazakhstan's Foreign Policy*), Almaty, Kazakhstan: Bilim, 1997.

6. See President Medvedev's address to Russian ambassadors at the Russian Foreign Ministry on July 12, 2010, available from *www.president.kremlin.ru*; and the publication of an internal MFA paper, K. Gaaze, M. Tsygar, *Rossiya Pomenyaet Vneshnyu Politiku* (*Russia Will Change Its Foreign Policy*), *Russian Newsweek*, Vol. 20, No. 288, 2010, available from *www.forbes.ru/ekonomika/vlast/49383-rossiya-pomenyaet-vneshnyuyu-politiku*. The author spoke about the need for a fundamental modernization of Russia's foreign policy in Dimitri Trenin, "Russia Reborn: Reimagining Moscow's Foreign Policy," *Foreign Affairs*, November-December 2009.

7. For a more detailed analysis of Russian attitudes toward Afghanistan, see Dmitri Trenin and Alexey Malashenko, *Afghanistan: A View from the North*, Washington, DC: Carnegie Endowment, 2010.

8. *World Drug Report 2010*, New York: United Nations, 2010, available from *www.unodc.org/documents/wdr/WDR_2010/World_Drug_Report_2010_lo-res.pdf*.

9. See Viktor Ivanov's speech at the Parliamentary Hearings in the State Duma of the Russian Federation, February 19, 2009, available from *www.fskn.gov.ru/includes/periodics/speeches_fskn/2009/0219/18014993/detail.shtml*.

10. Sergey Kulikov, *India I Pakistan Perekhodyat Dorogu Rossii* (*India and Pakistan Steal a March on Russia*), *Nezavisimaya gazeta*, April 15, 2008, available from *www.ng.ru/economics/2008-04-15/5_indipaki.html*.

11. See Dimitry Medvedev's Press Statement and Responses to Questions at News Conference following Russian-Italian In-

tergovernmental Consultations, Rome, Italy, December 3, 2009, available from *archive.kremlin.ru/eng/speeches/2009/12/03/1645_type82914type82915_223193.shtml.*

12. *Agreement between the Government of the Russian Federation and the Government of the United States of America on Transit of Weapons, Military Equipment, Military Assets and Personnel via Russian Federation Territory in Connection with Participation by Armed Forces of the United States of America in Efforts to Maintain Security, Stabilize and Rehabilitate the Islamic Republic of Afghanistan,* signed on July 6, 2009 in Moscow, Russia, available from *kremlin.ru/acts/10076.*

13. *World Drug Report - 2010.*

14. See Vladimir Putin's Meeting with Moscow Bureau Chiefs of Leading U.S. Media, Moscow, Russia, November 10, 2001, available from *archive.kremlin.ru/eng/text/speeches/2001/11/10/0001_type82915type82917type84779_143202.shtml.*

ABOUT THE CONTRIBUTORS

STEPHEN J. BLANK has served as the Strategic Studies Institute's expert on the Soviet bloc and the post-Soviet world since 1989. Prior to that he was Associate Professor of Soviet Studies at the Center for Aerospace Doctrine, Research, and Education, Maxwell Air Force Base, AL; and taught at the University of Texas, San Antonio; and at the University of California, Riverside. Dr. Blank is the editor of *Imperial Decline: Russia's Changing Position in Asia*, coeditor of *Soviet Military and the Future*, and author of *The Sorcerer as Apprentice: Stalin's Commissariat of Nationalities, 1917-1924*. He has also written many articles and conference papers on Russia, the Commonwealth of Independent States, and Eastern European security issues. Dr. Blank's current research deals with proliferation and the revolution in military affairs, and energy and security in Eurasia. His two most recent books are *Russo-Chinese Energy Relations: Politics in Command*, London, UK: Global Markets Briefing, 2006; and *Natural Allies? Regional Security in Asia and Prospects for Indo-American Strategic Cooperation*, Carlisle, PA: Strategic Studies Institute, U.S. Army War College, 2005. Dr. Blank holds a B.A. in history from the University of Pennsylvania, and an M.A. and Ph.D. in history from the University of Chicago.

SÉBASTIEN PEYROUSE is a Senior Research Fellow with the Central Asia-Caucasus Institute and Silk Road Studies Program, a Joint Center affiliated with Johns Hopkins University's School of Advanced International Studies, Washington, DC; and the Institute for Security and Development Policy in Stockholm, Sweden. His research originally focused on the impact of the Russian/Soviet heritage in the five Central Asian republics. His main areas of expertise are political systems in Central Asia, Islam and religious minorities, and Central Asia's geopolitical positioning toward China, Russia, and South Asia. In English, he has published *China as a Neighbor: Central Asian Perspectives and Strategies* (Central Asia-Caucasus Institute, 2009) with Marlène Laruelle; and "The Economic Aspects of the Chinese-Central-Asia Rapprochement" (Silk Road Papers, Central Asia-Caucasus Institute, 2007).

DIMITRI TRENIN is a senior associate of the Carnegie Endowment, the deputy director of the Carnegie Moscow Center, and chair of its Foreign and Security Policy Program. He has been with the Center since its inception in 1993. From 1993-97, Mr. Trenin held posts as a senior research fellow at the NATO Defense College in Rome, a visiting professor at the Free University of Brussels, and a senior research fellow at the Institute of Europe in Moscow. He served in the Soviet and Russian armed forces from 1972 to 1993, including experience working as a liaison officer in the External Relations Branch of the Group of Soviet Forces Germany, and as a staff member of the delegation to the U.S.-Soviet nuclear arms talks in Geneva from 1985 to 1991. He also taught at the Defense University in Moscow. Mr. Trenin authored *Getting Russia Right* (2007); *Russia's Restless Frontier: The Chechnya Factor in Post-Soviet Russia* (2004, with Aleksei V. Malashenko); and *The End of Eurasia: Russia on the Border Between Geopolitics and Globalization* (2001). He edited, with Steven Miller, *The Russian Military: Power and Policy* (2006).

www.ingramcontent.com/pod-product-compliance
Lightning Source LLC
Chambersburg PA
CBHW080208300326
41934CB00039B/3417